Contents

Acknowledgements

I would like to thank all at the Institute for Conflict Research for assisting me with this research, along with the Joseph Rowntree Charitable Trust, without whose funding this work would not have taken place. Furthermore, a special thanks to all of those who participated in the research, I hope that this research provides opportunities for new discussion on the impact of policing in Loyalist and Republican working class communities.

3703919595

UNIVERSITY OF
GLOUCESTERSHIRE
at Cheltenham and Gloucester

**FRANCIS CLOSE HALL
LEARNING CENTRE**

Swindon Road Cheltenham
Gloucestershire GL50 4AZ
Telephone: 01242 714600

NORMAL LOAN

Tel: 01242 714600

This publication was funded by the
Joseph Rowntree Charitable Trust.
The views expressed are not
necessarily those of the Trust.

First Published September 2008

Institute for Conflict Research
North City Business Centre
2 Duncairn Gardens
Belfast BT15 2GG
Tel: 028 9074 2682
Email: info@conflictresearch.org.uk
Web: www.conflictresearch.org.uk

ISBN 978-0-9552259-5-6

Produced by:
three creative company ltd

Executive Summary

This research project 'Policing in Loyalist and Republican communities: understanding key issues for local communities and the PSNI' was funded by the Joseph Rowntree Charitable Trust, and ran from August 2007 to June 2008. The central aim of the research was to explore Loyalist and Republican attitudes and concerns to policing within the context of the new political dispensation in Northern Ireland, and assess issues, concerns and hopes from the police in developing meaningful partnerships in these communities. The research consisted of a series of discussions with representatives from Nationalist/Republican communities, Unionist/Loyalist communities, representatives from District Policing Partnerships and the Northern Ireland Policing Board, PSNI representatives, and key informants (media, practitioners and academics). A number of themes emerged from these discussions that have been outlined below.

Nationalist/Republican

The legacy of policing through the conflict remains a sensitive an emotive issue for large sections of the Nationalist/Republican community. The majority of Nationalists and Republicans had limited experiences of policing, and that was usually confrontational. These communities were unable to identify with the policing and criminal justice system in a positive manner. However, there was an acknowledgement that in the ten years since the signing of The Good Friday Agreement society both required and deserved a modern and professional police service. The role of existing community safety and restorative justice programmes in supporting communities since Sinn Féin's endorsement of the PSNI cannot be understated. They have played a significant part in providing leadership and advice at the grass roots level by encouraging people to use the police and where appropriate facilitating engagement between the community and police.

Issues and complaints around the police now appeared to focus on response times, the flow of information and a lack of visible policing. There was an expectation that the police would deliver and address all of the communities' concerns of community safety and criminality. However, the realities of policing are very different. There is a slow realisation within some quarters that the police cannot resolve all of the issues, that a partnership approach is required, and that the community is central to this. The difficulty facing both the PSNI and local communities is how this partnership approach will operate in practice and determining the boundaries between the community taking a responsibility for policing and the PSNI fulfilling their roles and responsibilities.

Unionist/Loyalist

There is a minimal amount of research that documents the perceptions of the Unionist/Loyalist communities towards the police and also their levels of engagement and participation in policing led programmes and initiatives. From the discussions it became apparent that the legacy of the conflict had a significant impact on how these communities viewed the police. There was a fragmentation within Loyalist communities during the conflict with those supporting paramilitaries disengaging with the formal criminal justice system. Those that remained but did not support Loyalist paramilitaries were encouraged not to engage with the police or develop any meaningful forms of relationships.

One consequence was the movement of police officers away from the Loyalist working class communities. The knock-on effect was that these communities began to lose their affiliation and identity with the police, along with an argument that the police could not identify with the issues and concerns that were prevalent within working class communities as they did not reside within them. This, compounded with the policing of parades and the political changes, has led to a complete disengagement in some communities with the police.

Positive experiences of policing are at a minimum, and there is some suspicion from some sections of Loyalism that the interests of their communities are being left behind in pursuit of the support and endorsement of the Republican communities for policing. There have been attempts to develop relationships and build positive partnerships, but these have come from the community and are largely built upon personalities and specific individuals. There does not appear to be a coherent strategy of engagement from the police in relation to building associations and links with Loyalist working class communities.

PSNI

The police have undergone a number of structural, operational and more importantly organisational changes in the last decade. Considering their role throughout the conflict and the injuries and loss of life experienced by the police it has proved an emotive and sensitive period in their history. However, there was an acknowledgement that the police had to change and adapt to the new social and political climate evident within Northern Ireland. Post-ceasefire policing is very different to policing during the conflict. There is a stronger emphasis on building and sustaining relationships and forging new partnerships with communities and different statutory agencies. However, there was also a realisation that this was to take place within the context of decreasing resources, increased community expectations, and continued threats and attacks from dissident Republicans and elements from within Loyalist communities.

It was apparent that the police recognised the need to develop positive working partnerships in the community. They understood the importance of the existing community-based initiatives and programmes and these appeared compatible with the workings of the formal criminal justice system. However, these partnerships were relatively new and still in their infancy. The boundaries between the communities' ownership of community safety programmes and initiatives and the role of the PSNI has yet to be established or more importantly tested. What is clear is that there is a realisation from the police that they alone do not hold the key to addressing criminality and anti-social behaviour. Instead a multi-agency approach with strong community participation is necessary for dealing with and responding to these incidents.

The new relationships with the Republican community were welcomed, although it was noted the potential impact this community would have on existing capacity and resources. The police often referred to the lack of resources and there was a hint of hesitancy from officers about meeting this community's expectations while their numbers continue to decrease. Discussions on the implementation and delivery of community policing received mixed responses. It became apparent that at a strategic level it was not receiving enough support or direction. Communities were keen for engagement and discussions to take place, but it appeared that organisationally community policing was often sacrificed for more measurable targets.

DPP and Policing Board

The DPP members, both independent and elected, highlighted the potential positive role that the partnerships could have in relation to developing relationships between the police and local communities. However, there was an acknowledgement that the majority of the general public were unsure of the roles and responsibilities of a DPP member.

This was reflected in the poor attendance at the majority of public meetings. There had been recorded instances where no members of the public attended the meetings.

A further criticism of the DPP from the independent members centred on the attendance and contribution of a number of elected representatives of the partnerships. There was a general consensus that they were not supporting the process or contributing in a positive and meaningful manner. Questions were raised as to the role of the NIPB in managing and monitoring the roles of the DPP. There did not appear to be adequate monitoring of members' attendance at public and private meetings. Nor were there appropriate mechanisms in place to assess the impact DPPs were having in both monitoring the PSNI at a local level, but more importantly facilitating relationships between the community and the police. Several members also questioned the willingness of the PSNI to engage with DPPs. A number of members had experiences where the police appeared not to be interested in the benefits of DPPs and viewed them as a hindrance and obstacle to policing.

Summary

The findings revealed the deep-rooted sensitivities that continue to surround the area of policing and justice. However, all the main protagonists recognised both the symbolic and practical benefits of having a police service that is endorsed by all of the political parties and is acceptable to the majority of local communities. Republicans, Loyalists and the police have all undergone significant changes in recent years and have had to adapt to a new social and political environment. They have become the central figures in this new chapter of policing and justice.

1. Introduction

The topic of policing, security and justice has dominated the social and political environment in Northern Ireland since the first paramilitary ceasefires in 1994. Within the context of Northern Ireland's history one would be hard placed to think of a more emotive, controversial, and sensitive topic (Mulcahy, 2006). It is an area that has divided opinion between Nationalist/Republican and Unionist/Loyalist communities for decades. However in recent years there have been a number of significant events that have impacted on policing including the signing of the Agreement (1998), the publication of the Patten Report (1999), the devolution of powers to the Stormont Assembly (1999), the formation of the PSNI (2001), the final decommissioning of Republican weapons (2005), power sharing by Sinn Féin and the Democratic Unionist Party (2007), and Sinn Féin endorsing the policing and criminal justice structures (2008). These events have provided practical evidence of the distance Northern Ireland has travelled in the last decade. In the current political climate, debates are now dominated by the date for the devolution of policing and justice powers from Westminster to Stormont. This is viewed by large sections of the community as a key milestone that would provide further tangible evidence that Northern Ireland has progressed as a post-conflict society.

This research is primarily concerned with examining the central issues and concerns prevalent within Loyalist and Republican communities in relation to policing and criminal justice. It is set within a context where there has been a minimal amount of research into the impact of policing within these communities. So much of the research around policing in the past has been set within a framework where paramilitary organisations have continued to influence the state governance and security policy. However, this report has an opportunity to examine issues that are unrelated to the conflict and focus on policing within a post-conflict environment, which is being steered under the distinct theme of 'policing with the community'. The idea of 'policing with the community' can be found within several of the 175 recommendations contained within the Patten Report. Recommendation 44 states that *'Policing with the Community should be the core function of the police service and the core function of every police station'* (pg.43). Furthermore, it was hoped that these recommendations would fundamentally alter the relationship between the police and community and establish policing as a *'collective responsibility'* with policing as a matter for the whole community, not something that the *'community leaves the police to do'*

(Smyth, 2002). A key element of this research is to determine how much of this idea is actually a reality and practically being implemented and how much of it remains an idealistic vision.

The problems associated with poor engagement between communities and the police first came to prominence in the USA in the early 1970s (Bennett-Sandler, 1979). However, community policing first came to the fore in England and Wales in the early 1980s after the publication of the Scarman Report (1981) that examined the riots in a number of British cities. The report recommended that there should be greater community involvement in the formulation of policing policy and police operations (Reiner, 1995). Furthermore, it recommended that the police develop structures (local liaison committees), forums and committees in an attempt to encourage greater community participation in policing issues and to also facilitate relationship building between the police and local communities. Community policing is about being proactive as opposed to reactive, and about positive service delivery, partnership working, problem solving and accountability. There are critics of community policing who see it as a philosophy, as opposed to a programme, which lacks substance and is difficult to define and measure. They maintain that the ambiguity of the concept has meant that any type of police tactics can be labelled as 'community policing' (Rosenbaum and Lurigio, 2000)

The recommendations from the Patten Report provided both the police and local communities with an opportunity to build new relationships and address community issues and concerns within a multi-agency framework where the response was designed to fit the need. According to the PSNI:

Community policing is proactive, solution-based and community driven. It occurs where the police and law-abiding citizens work to do four things: prevent crime, inter-agency problem solving, bring offenders to justice, and improve the overall quality of life (PSNI, 2002).

The policy of 'policing with the community' has been a central element of policing practice since the establishment of the PSNI. However, it is unclear how the realities of community policing have impacted within Loyalist and Republican working class communities since Sinn Féin and the wider Republican community endorsed the policing structures and began practical engagement. A key aspect of this report is to examine the relationship between these communities and the police and determine whether the community policing that Patten envisaged is actually being delivered in a practical and meaningful manner.

Methodology

This research project 'Policing in Loyalist and Republican communities: understanding key issues for local communities and the PSNI' was funded by the Joseph Rowntree Charitable Trust, and ran from August 2007 to June 2008. The research was conducted at a significant time, as Northern Ireland had only recently established a devolved administration (Powell, 2007) involving the two dominant political parties and long term rivals Sinn Féin and the Democratic Unionist Party. Furthermore, for the first time in the history of Northern Ireland all of the main Nationalist/Republican, Unionist/Loyalist political parties had formally engaged with all elements of the formal criminal justice system.

The central aim of the research was to explore Loyalist and Republican attitudes and concerns to policing within the context of the new political dispensation in Northern Ireland. The four main objectives were to:

1. Explore the current attitudes to policing in the two communities and create a mechanism where debate and discussion could take place around the nature of policing and justice within each community; highlight current and future perceptions and concerns about policing and detail how existing community based community safety initiatives could be incorporated into formal policing strategies;
2. Highlight the perceptions of policing in any future devolved administration from the viewpoint of Loyalist and Republican communities. Document the concerns and issues for not acknowledging or supporting the current policing structures in Northern Ireland;
3. Consider how Loyalist and Republican communities might incorporate their current activities and community safety strategies into the formal policing system and explore how this process will take place. This may build on existing developments in incorporating community based restorative justice projects into the wider criminal justice system; and,
4. Explore the attitudes within the PSNI to the challenges that the police will face in developing a more inclusive policing process and in engaging effectively with erstwhile antagonistic communities. This will include both discussions at senior local management level and among lower ranking officers.

Methods

The research involved a series of discussions through informal and formal interviews, focus groups and in-depth conversations with representatives from Nationalist/Republican communities, Unionist/Loyalist communities, DPPs and Policing Board members, PSNI representatives and key informants. The discussions primarily took place with individuals from the Greater Belfast and Derry/Londonderry areas. These areas were selected for the large number of Loyalist and Republican working class communities and the various community safety programmes that had been developed at the grass roots level within these areas.

Nationalist/Republican respondents: These included political representatives; community representatives; local residents; ex-prisoners; and individuals involved in community safety initiatives. Discussions focused on a number of topics including, the historical and contemporary perceptions of policing; local attitudes and experiences of policing; the expectations of policing; views on the compatibility of community mechanisms of safety and justice within the criminal justice system; and future methods of building partnerships between the community and the police.
.

Unionist/Loyalist respondents: These included political representatives; community representatives; local residents; ex-prisoners; and individuals involved in community safety initiatives. Discussions focused on a number of topics including, the communities' relationship and experience of policing; the realities of current policing practice; local community safety initiatives; the role of paramilitaries in policing communities; and the perceived lack of political support for Loyalist communities in debates around policing.

PSNI Officers from both strategic and operation levels: These included officers from management level; officers at District Command level; and officers from Neighbourhood Teams and Community Safety. Discussions focused on a number of topics including the various strategies involved in community engagement and community policing; the issues facing police; policing in Loyalist and Republican communities; community expectations of policing, along with police expectations for the future of policing.

District Policing Partnership Members/Policing Board Members: These included independent and elected members, DPP staff, and

Policing Board members and staff. A number of themes were used to guide these discussions including the impact of devolved government on criminal justice issues; the mechanisms for developing relationships between local communities and the police; issues and concerns in relation to community policing; and the future outlook for policing.

Key informants: These included members of the media, practitioners, academics and those with a specific interest in policing and criminal justice. These conversations incorporated a number of the themes from above, and provided an opportunity to reflect on existing findings and examine different perspectives of policing.

Fieldwork

This project offered a unique opportunity to develop an understanding of the key issues that exist in relation to policing in Loyalist and Republican communities. Accessing members of the PSNI, NIPB and DPP to contribute to the research proved relatively uncomplicated. Each organisation upon an initial meeting facilitated further discussions with representatives from their respective organisations/departments. However, gaining an insight into the views and concerns of those from Loyalist and Republican communities proved slightly more difficult as this remained a sensitive and controversial topic within these communities. At the beginning it was difficult to broach the topic of policing with community representatives. However, through time and by attending a number of community meetings and participating in conversations around community issues, the topic eventually steered its way onto policing. Developing close relationships with community representatives from both Loyalist and Republican areas allowed for positive interaction with members from their communities. It was initially decided to record all of the discussions for the research. However, it soon became apparent that a significant number of individuals from the community were reluctant to be taped, so note taking became the main method of recording.

Summary

To understand the complexity of policing and its role throughout the course of the Troubles, it is important to gain an insight into the history of policing within the context of Northern Ireland. It will become apparent that history and events are viewed very differently depending entirely on the particular community background one comes from. The following chapter will chart the development of policing from the partition of Ireland in 1921 to the present day. Chapter three will focus on the various community based-initiatives that sprang up in Loyalist and Republican communities to combat issues of anti-social and criminal behaviour. Chapters four, five, six and seven contain the main findings from the discussions with Nationalists/Republicans, Unionists/Loyalists, the PSNI and District Policing Partnership and Policing Board members respectively. The report then concludes with Chapter eight which outlines the key findings and emerging themes from the discussions.

2. RUC to the PSNI

The following chapter provides a historical analysis of the key events that have impacted on policing in Northern Ireland since partition in 1921. These include the emergence of the RUC; the impact of the Troubles on policing; the role of the British Army in Northern Ireland; changes and reforms to policing and security; the Patten Report and finally the decision by Republicans to recognise and endorse the legitimacy of the new policing structures.

Policing 1921-1968

The Royal Ulster Constabulary was established in June 1922 (Ryder, 2000), a year after the Anglo-Irish Treaty of 1921, which established the Northern Ireland state. The Northern Ireland government was exclusively Protestant/Unionist and had sole responsibility over security, policing and law and order in Northern Ireland. From the outset the RUC was shrouded in controversy, with Nationalists viewing it as a paramilitary force created to maintain a Unionist state, and Unionists recognising the RUC as their police force, tasked with defending their rights within the context of the newly established state (McGarry and O'Leary, 1999). Further tensions between Nationalists and Unionists emerged over the composition of the RUC. It was suggested that one third of the force should consist of members of the Catholic community in order to be more representative of the population it policed. However, at its peak in early 1923, Catholics constituted 21 per cent of the RUC, which declined to 10 per cent by 1966 (Weitzer, 1995). Unlike other police forces in the United Kingdom, the RUC were allowed to carry arms, and had access to wide range of 'special' powers laid down in legislation enacted by the Unionist government. These centred around arrest, search, questioning, detention, and internment (Ellison and Smyth, 2000). Although the RUC was established under the premise of conducting 'normal' policing, ultimately this role incorporated a number of tasks with a political element:

From its inception, the RUC was a paramilitary force and one that played a highly political role...While the RUC undoubtedly performed 'routine' policing duties, these were ultimately subjugated to its primary role for the suppression of Nationalist dissent (Ellison and Smyth, 2000).

A further force separate from the RUC and responsible for security and policing in Northern Ireland was the Ulster Special Constabulary (USC).

This was an auxiliary police force formed in 1920 to defend Northern Ireland from attacks by the Irish Republican Army (IRA):

They were a large, armed voluntary force responsible for manning roadblocks, patrolling along the border, assisting in riot control, and guarding buildings at night (Weitzer, 1995).

The force initially consisted of full-time, part-time, and reserve sections, known respectively as A, B, and C sections. In 1925 sections A and C were disbanded, leaving only the B Specials, as a largely part-time reserve force, to support the regular RUC. Its membership was almost entirely made up of members of the Protestant community. Accordingly, it was held in high esteem by Unionists but criticised vigorously by Nationalists (Gillespie, 2008).

Throughout the 1930s, 40s and 50s Northern Ireland enjoyed a period of relative stability, despite Catholic and Nationalist criticism of the RUC and repeated incidents of discrimination and physical abuse (Weitzer, 1995). Over this period there were riots and public disturbances, and on occasions the IRA directed acts of violence against the RUC and B Specials, yet from the mid-1920s through to 1968 only 18 deaths occurred because of political or inter-ethnic conflict (Rose, 1976). However, a number of events in 1968 and 1969 were to provide the catalyst for thirty years of violence, known as the 'Troubles', which shaped policing and security policies in Northern Ireland for over a generation.

The onset of the Troubles

By 1968 Northern Ireland was in the throws of an extensive civil rights campaign, which was predominantly headed up by members of the Nationalist community. The campaign was modelled on the civil rights campaign in the United States of America, involving protests, marches, sit-ins and the use of the media to publicise minority grievances. Nationalist campaigners argued for a more equitable access to political power, social provision and cultural recognition. As MacGinty and Darby (2002) noted, politics eventually spilled onto the streets with demonstrations and counter-demonstrations by members of the Nationalist and Unionist communities. The international media became extremely interested with events in Northern Ireland, and their coverage of three very public incidents inadvertently shaped the future of policing in Northern Ireland. In October 1968 the RUC attacked civil rights demonstrators in Derry/Londonderry; in January 1969 a number of

Loyalists, including members of the RUC (McGarry and O'Leary, 1999), ambushed a civil rights march at Burntollet Bridge; and finally in August 1969 the RUC and B Specials clashed with Catholic/Nationalist protesters in Derry/Londonderry in an incident that became known as the 'Battle of the Bogside'. There were two key outcomes from these events. Firstly, many Nationalists' perceptions of the RUC as the armed wing of the Unionist government, who colluded with the loyalist community to restrict Nationalist demonstrations against the state, were reinforced and vindicated (Weitzer, 1995). Secondly, the British government in the face of international criticism, and with a degree of reluctance, decided to deploy the army into Northern Ireland *'in aid of the civil power'* (Mulcahy, 2006). On the 14th August 1969, soldiers from the Prince of Wales Own Regiment went on duty in Derry/Londonderry.

A number of enquiries were conducted in the wake of the civil unrest and sectarian violence and disorder. The Cameron Report (1969) and Scarman Tribunal (1972) made a number of criticisms of the RUC and the B Specials in relation to their use of force, behaviour and differential treatment of Nationalist and Unionist communities. As Scarman noted, the police response to the Civil Rights Movement had created what he gravely termed *'the fateful split'* between the Nationalist community and the police (Mulcahy, 2006). It became apparent to the British government that significant changes had to be introduced into the RUC to address the concerns of the Nationalist community. In response, the Hunt Committee (1969) was established to examine the policing structures and security apparatus within Northern Ireland (Ryder, 2000).

The Hunt Report (1969) recommended widespread reforms to the security forces, including the disarming of the RUC, the creation of an RUC Reserve, and replacement of the B Specials by a part-time force under the command of the British Army. The Ulster Defence Regiment, (UDR) as it was formally known, consisted of part and full time members and was tasked with guarding installations and conducting patrols that included roadblocks and house searches. It was a predominantly Protestant organisation, with only 3 per cent of its members being from the Catholic community in 1991.

A further recommendation from Hunt was for the formation of an independent Police Authority. This was intended to oversee the RUC in a more neutral fashion than the previous Home Affairs Ministry. It was established in 1970. From the outset the mechanism of accountability was questioned. It was criticised for not being an elected body; boycotted by Nationalist and Republican political parties; and generally regarded as having minimal or no powers to bring the RUC to account (O'Rawe and Moore, 1997). Overall the Hunt Report was critical of the system of policing, particularly its paramilitary image and character, and its security role (McGarry and O'leary, 1999). The report was welcomed by the Nationalist community, but drew criticism from the Unionist community. It should be noted that the first RUC officer killed in the Troubles was shot by a member of a Loyalist paramilitary group during public riots over the publication of the Hunt Report in Belfast on the 11th October 1969 (Ryder, 2000).

The majority of Hunt's proposals were endorsed by the British government and the modernizing and normalization of the RUC had begun. However, it is important to note that the practical changes envisaged by Hunt were to be viewed within the context of a peaceful society, one with limited or no paramilitary and/or sectarian violence. Initially the RUC were disarmed, and significant reforms were adopted. However, this was short lived, and as the security situation deteriorated the RUC were re-armed in October 1971. Furthermore, the British Army continued to have a significant presence on the streets of Northern Ireland. After initially being welcomed within Nationalist communities, the army were soon portrayed as an aggressive force, protecting the interests of the Unionist government. From 1970 to 1976 the British Army replaced the RUC as the premier security force responsible for street patrols, house searches, intelligence gathering, and riot control (Weitzer, 1995). Throughout this period there were a number of key events involving the security forces that both exacerbated and escalated the violence, which in turn required a stronger security response, which ultimately eroded Nationalist confidence in all of the policing and justice structures.

Increased violence

In August 1971, the Unionist government introduced internment in the face of rising Republican violence. In the four years it was operational 1,981 people were detained. Of these, 107 were Loyalist, and the rest were regarded as Republicans (Gillespie, 2008). In retrospect, internment was viewed as a disaster, as they detained too many people who had no previous associations with paramilitary organisations, which did not quell the violence and disorder, and instead provided the catalyst for more violence and positive propaganda for the IRA. To compound matters, the events on Bloody Sunday, 30th January 1972, were to have an even more significant effect on the management and administration of policing and justice in Northern Ireland when the British Army shot dead fourteen unarmed civilians at a banned anti-internment march in Derry/Londonderry. In response to this incident, as Mulcahy (2006) notes, the British government demanded control over the security forces. The Unionist government initially refused and in protest resigned from office. The Northern Ireland parliament was suspended and Direct Rule was imposed from Westminster (Ryder, 2000; Ellison, 2000; Tomlinson, 1993).

Throughout the 1970s the IRA stepped up its campaign of violence, targeting members of the RUC, British Army and the newly established UDR. Until 1976 the RUC played a subordinate role to the army in security policy and action but continued to suffer heavy casualties (McGarry and O'Leary, 1999). However, in 1976 the British government adopted a new policy following an internal review of the security situation in Northern Ireland (Gardiner Committee, 1975). This concluded that the military approach had failed, and that there should be a shift of responsibility back to the RUC. According to Weitzer (1995) the logic behind this was to redefine the nature of the conflict. Existing security mechanisms gave credence to the Republican claims that they were engaged in a war, the new policy of criminalisation was based upon a redefinition of the conflict as a law and order problem. This was to be implemented by the police and courts. This shift in security policy was referred to as 'Police Primacy' and/or 'Ulsterisation' (Mulcahy, 2006).

In 1976 the RUC resumed sole responsibility for security, law and order within Northern Ireland, with the army playing a supporting role. One consequence of this new policy was the expanded role of the RUC and the subsequent increase in numbers of police officers. The RUC had to dramatically increase its capacity to address the threats of Loyalist and Republican paramilitaries, and also engage in 'normal' policing operations expected of a civil police force (Tomlinson, 1993). By 1979, the army had reduced troop levels by 4,000 to 13,000, while the RUC had increased by 4,000 to just over 7,000 officers, and the UDR totalled 2,400 full-time members, with the total number of security personnel within Northern Ireland being approximately 22,000 (Tomlinson, 1993).

The significance of the advent of the policy of 'Police Primacy' cannot be understated. Mulcahy (2006) suggests that the new measures reflected a significant shift in the security policy for Northern Ireland, not least in terms of the professionalisation of the RUC. It redefined the conflict in terms of who were the main protagonists and the purpose of the violence. Furthermore it forced wider sections of the Nationalist community to reassess their views of the conflict. The terminology and language became less militaristic, and the British government attempted to convince large sections of the media that this was an internal, local issue of law and order. The other aspect of 'Police Primacy' was to effect changes within the RUC. There was recognition from the British government that the lack of legitimacy for the RUC from the wider Nationalist population had to be addressed. This required a shift towards the professionalisation of policing in terms of impartiality, accountability and consent (Mulcahy and Ellison, 2001). Developments throughout the 1980s and early 1990s reflected this new policy including the publication of the 'RUC's Professional Policing Ethics' (1988), the 'RUC's Statement of Purpose and Values' (1992) and the 'RUC Charter' (1993). There was a growing awareness within the organisation of ethics, good behaviour practice and positive service delivery (Mulcahy, 2006). However, it wasn't until the paramilitary cease-fires in 1994 that the policing and security structures had an opportunity to reflect on the possibility of policing within a 'normal' context. This will be explored in more detail further on in the chapter.

Nationalist/Republican criticisms

Large sections of the Nationalist/Republican communities refused to support or engage with the policing and security structures throughout the duration of the Troubles. There were a number of explanations for this attitude. There was a genuine belief that the police were openly discriminatory against Nationalists and that they often used excessive force and threatening behaviour simply because of their community background. Furthermore, a major reality of the Troubles was that members of the Nationalist/Republican communities were encouraged not to recognise the legitimacy of the RUC. In fact members of those same communities were threatened, intimidated, attacked and murdered if they joined the state security forces or facilitated their role in policing the community (Taylor, 1999).

There was also a strongly held view that the policing structures were not representative or inclusive, and failed to recognise the interests of the Nationalist community:

Many in the RUC, and virtually all of the B Specials were defenders of the Protestant community first, defenders of the Protestant state second, and normal policemen third (Ruane and Todd, 1996).

Catholics and Nationalists have consistently regarded the police as looking more favourably towards Protestants and Unionists. There was a widely held belief that the RUC and other security agencies focused most of their attention on Nationalist/Republican communities. Nationalists were disproportionately searched, arrested and convicted compared to members of the Unionist community. Furthermore, Nationalists were disproportionately the victims of plastic bullets and baton rounds fired by both the British Army and the RUC (Mulcahy, 2006).

Throughout the Troubles there was a general consensus from those in the Nationalist community that the RUC was overwhelmingly Protestant in numbers, image and ethos. Research by Brewer and Magee (1991) noted that a large number of police officers read Protestant newspapers, supported Protestant soccer teams, and shared the general outlook of the Protestant community, including presumably its political views. This is further reinforced through the work of Ellison (1998) who concluded that *'the locker room banter, or 'canteen culture', in the RUC was profoundly anti-Catholic'*. There was a large amount of evidence to suggest that the names, symbols and icons attached to the RUC were, for the most part, solidly Unionist. The dominance of the Protestant and Unionist culture assists in explaining not only why a large section of the Nationalist community did not join the RUC, but also why a considerable amount were unable to identify or engage with it (McGarry and O'Leary, 1999).

There was also criticism of the wider criminal justice system, with specific attention focused on the Diplock courts. These were given this name after a government commission in 1972 under Lord Diplock concluded that non-jury trials should be used in cases relating to terrorist offences. The argument was based on the premise that juries risked threats and intimidation in terrorist trials. Those brought before the courts felt that they were being tried in an unfair, biased system with one individual being 'judge, jury and sentencer'. The other major concern from Nationalists/Republicans was the use of 'supergrasses' by the RUC. By the early 1980s, the RUC had cultivated the 'supergrass', a paramilitary member who would implicate large numbers of colleagues in return for a new identity, relocation and financial reward (Greer and Whyte, 1986). However, in the years after supergrass trials, fifteen out of twenty five cases collapsed when the key witnesses retracted their statements. As McGarry and O'Leary (1999) noted, this did nothing for Catholic or Nationalist impressions of the police or the judicial system in general.

Further instances of policing that alienated large sections of the Nationalist community revolved around allegations of a shoot-to-kill policy (Stalker, 1988) along with RUC/UDR collusion with Loyalist paramilitary groups (PONI, 2007). Throughout the conflict there were a number of claims that the security forces had adopted a policy of shoot-to-kill. This came to the fore in 1982 following the killing of six Catholic men by the RUC. A subsequent inquiry conducted by Stalker was concluded in controversial circumstances, with no prosecutions arising from the inquiry on the grounds of national security (Gillespie, 2008). The incident and the subsequent investigation did nothing to encourage Nationalist confidence in the RUC.

For a number of years there have been claims that security forces colluded with Loyalist paramilitary organisations (Human Rights Watch/ Helsinki, 1991; Dillon, 1991). In 1989 the Stevens Inquiry was established to assess how security information came to Loyalist paramilitaries (Stevens Report, 2003). The investigation concluded that there had been collusion between the security forces and Loyalist paramilitaries, but that it was on an individual basis and was not institutionalised. There have been a number of high profile murders with allegations of collusion including Pat Finucane killed in 1989, Raymond McCord Jr. in 1997, and Rosemary Nelson in 1999. Recently, the Police Ombudsman for Northern Ireland (2007) published a report on collusion and concluded that Special Branch officers protected Loyalist paramilitary informants and failed to stop them committing up to fifteen murders. Collectively the negative experiences of policing, along with the perceptions of discrimination and bias and the public revelations of collusion and the recruitment of informers, influenced Nationalist and Republican views of policing in Northern Ireland.

Paramilitary ceasefires

There is no definitive agreement on when the Troubles first started or when they concluded, or the total number of fatalities that resulted from the conflict (Gillespie, 2008). Apportioning responsibility for incidents and providing a definitive number of casualties as a result of the conflict is both sensitive and often controversial. However, McKittrick et al, (2007) concluded that from June 1966 to May 2006 there were 3,720 deaths, 3,453 of which occurred in Northern Ireland. Paramilitary organisations suffered 562 deaths, the security forces 1,039 and 2,119 civilians were killed. The Royal Ulster Constabulary lost a total of 302 officers from 1969 to 2001 with a further 8,500 injured. The RUC was also responsible for approximately 51 deaths with a further 316 attributed to the British Army and other agencies affiliated to the security forces. Republican paramilitaries were responsible for 2,152 deaths and Loyalists were accountable for 1,112 deaths (Gillespie, 2008).

On the 31st August 1994 the Provisional IRA declared 'a complete cessation of military operations'. The main Loyalist paramilitary organisations declared a ceasefire on the 13th October 1994. Prior to the ceasefires there were intensive political discussions involving the British and Irish governments, along with the local Nationalist and Republican political parties. The conclusion of paramilitary violence brought immediate rewards with the relaxation of a number of security measures (MacGinty and Darby, 2002). There was a significant decrease in the number of roadblocks and security checkpoints, and a reduction in the military presence on the ground. There was a realisation from the security forces that a long-term strategy had to be developed in relation to the delivery of 'normal policing' in a post-conflict society. The RUC undertook an internal review to determine how a permanent peace in Northern Ireland would affect the role, structure and style of policing (RUC, 1996). It was interesting to note that a number of recommendations that emerged from the Fundamental Review of Policing (1996) were later produced in the Patten Report (1999).

Patten Report

In 1998, approximately four years after the first paramilitary ceasefire the main Nationalist and Unionist political parties, along with the Irish and British governments, successfully negotiated the Agreement (1998). The Agreement contained proposals for both a political and a peace settlement, dealing with constitutional issues along with prisoner releases, north-south bodies, issues of consent, and the structures necessary for the establishment of a local devolved government. Ryder (2000) has indicated that policing was one of the most contentious issues at the Stormont negotiations. Furthermore McGarry and O'Leary (1999) note:

Police reform in Northern Ireland is at the organisational heart of the national conflict between Nationalists and Unionists and Republicans and Loyalists…police reform was such a heated subject in the making of the agreement that it was decided to postpone it.

The Agreement called for an independent commission to be established to inquire into policing in Northern Ireland and to make recommendations for future policing structures and arrangements. Chris Patten was tasked with chairing the committee and finally reported their findings in September 1999, fifteen months after their consultation had begun. The primary purpose of the Patten Report was to apply the consociational principles of the Agreement to create a representative policing structure, which could claim support from the broader communities in Northern Ireland.

The Patten Report itself had a dual function which was essentially the reform and demilitarisation of the police. As policing in Northern Ireland had become preoccupied with counter-terrorism, the Patten Report was commissioned to develop policing towards a model which shared features similar to its Anglo-Saxon policing counterparts, concerned with the core principles of community-based policing, focused on crime prevention, order maintenance and local participation. As Patten noted at the launch of the report:

Policing in Northern Ireland has suffered, often with disastrous consequences, from being a political issue and from being associated with the debate about the state itself (Irish News: 10.09.99).

The Patten Report contained 175 recommendations for policing in Northern Ireland (Patten, 1999). The two central principles that underpin the recommendations are human rights, and the relationship between the police and the public (Mulcahy, 2006). The report recommended the introduction of *'a comprehensive programme of action to focus policing in Northern Ireland on a human rights-based approach'.* As for policing with the community, the Patten Report noted that *'policing should be a collective community responsibility: a partnership for community safety'.*

The Patten Commission was also charged with recommending what has since become an extensive complex of accountability structures, designed to oversee the process of transformation of the police and to ensure the administration of an accountable and effective police service. The Office of the Oversight Commissioner, seen as a temporary measure, was the first line in this structure. It has been responsible for overseeing the implementation of the changes in policing arrangements and structures, in the context of the 175 recommendations of the Patten Report. It was the Commissioner's responsibility to:

Monitor and review progress achieved in implementing change; receive reports, information and explanations, as required, from the agencies responsible for progress; and provide public assurance about the progress of the implementation process (Patten Report, 1999).

The Patten Report also advocated an additional triumvirate of organisations that were established to monitor the ongoing effectiveness of the PSNI and hold it to democratic account beyond the expiration of the function of the Oversight Commissioner. These included the Policing Board, which holds the Chief Constable to account and sets out policing priorities. Patten also recommended that each of the twenty six District

Council areas should establish a District Policing Partnership (DPP) whose membership should consist of both elected and independent representatives. The DPPs provide the local level of accountability for policing, facilitating the interface between communities and the police service. The Police Ombudsman provides the third and final arm in overseeing the accountability of the police force, and was established through the Police (Northern Ireland) Act 1998 in order to replace the controversial Independent Commission for Police Complaints. Independent of the PSNI, the Police Ombudsman can be considered the primary mechanism of ensuring accountability regarding the day-to-day practices and behaviours of the police service. The Ombudsman has the powers to investigate complaints made by citizens but also to investigate any area that it feels may involve police misconduct or may be of interest to the Secretary of State.

Support for Patten

The implementation of the Patten Report was to face two immediate substantial obstacles. The first was the negative Unionist reaction to the report with a coalition of interested parties (Ellison, 1998) being established to resist any fundamental changes to the RUC. These included all of the main Unionist political parties, the ex-Chief Constable Sir John Hermon, the Orange Order, the Police Federation Northern Ireland (PFNI), and the media (Daily Telegraph). The second obstacle was Nationalist and Republic anger at the partial implementation of Patten's recommendations in the Police (Northern Ireland) Act 2000, with specific criticism attached to the reduced powers of the Policing Board, and the reduced authority and responsibility given to the DPPs.

Unionists were resistant and critical towards the recommended changes to policing. Much of their opposition was targeted towards the more 'superficial' aspect of change, particularly the symbolic elements rather than the more lengthy recommendations of structural and organisational reform. Their two key arguments for a continuation of the RUC focused on the premise that a significant number of Catholics support the RUC, and that the symbolic trappings of policing, uniform, insignia and the flying of the Union Jack, offered no threat to the Nationalist identity, but were in fact shared by everyone (Mulcahy, 2006).

On the other hand Nationalists and Republicans were more inclined to look favourably on the recommendations from Patten. The SDLP and Sinn Féin by 2000 were actively calling for the full implementation of all

175 recommendations. They were particularly in favour of the recommended 50:50 recruiting, which was aimed at boosting the considerable deficit of Catholics in the police force, which stood at 8.3 per cent in 1998, despite Catholics composing 43 per cent of the population.

There were a number of debates, public rallies and campaigns set up in the aftermath of the publication of the Patten Report (Mulcahy, 2006). The Police Federation of Northern Ireland launched a petition and amassed 400,000 signatures supporting the RUC against the Patten recommendations. The British government reviewed the Patten Report and decided upon implementing a number but not all of the recommendations in the Police (Northern Ireland) Act 2000. The government initially came under a degree of criticism from both Nationalists and a number of the authors of the Patten Report for what they called 'diluting' the initial recommendations (Ryder, 2000). Criticisms centred on a lack of legislation to allow ex-prisoners to sit on DPPs, reduced powers for the Oversight Commissioner, reduced accountability measures for the Policing Board, and a reduced emphasis on Human Rights. However, the policing debate continued. Neither the SDLP nor Sinn Féin supported the 2000 Act which contained the watered down recommendations. Further discussions were held, with negotiations involving the main political parties and the two governments. The outcomes from the Weston Park talks (2001) resulted in the Police (Northern Ireland) Act 2003. This Act had a stronger emphasis on the idea of 'policing with the community'. These changes satisfied the SDLP who immediately engaged with the new policing structures, the Policing Board and the DPPs. However, Sinn Féin remained unwilling to endorse the new policing structures.

Unionist/Loyalist perceptions

There has been a widely held belief from Nationalists that Unionists and Loyalists are supportive of the various policing and security mechanisms deployed within Northern Ireland. However, this has not always been the case, with levels of engagement and participation poor within some sections of the Loyalist community. According to McGloin (2003), over the course of the Troubles Northern Ireland lacked a universally acceptable police force, which has left a vacuum of authority in certain Loyalist and Republican communities. Therefore focusing purely on Nationalist/Republican frustrations with the police overlooks the trend of increasing loyalist isolation from the police in Northern Ireland. The Patten Report (1999) indicated that:

In the lower income groups, Protestants could be as strongly alienated from the police as their Catholic counterparts.

Loyalist criticism of the police predated the Agreement (1998) and the subsequent transformation of the police from the RUC to the PSNI (2001). There had been a number of events, such as the policing of the Anglo-Irish Agreement (AIA) in 1985:

The RUC's willingness to face down anti AIA protests shocked many staunch unionists and loyalists...the RUC continued to "hold the line" but at considerable cost to its relations with the unionist community (Ryder, 2000).

Contentious parades such as Drumcree in the 1990s (Bryan, 2000), and policing in working class areas in general, have led to a perceived notion within Loyalist communities, that they were now being treated worse than, or no better than, Catholics (Dunn and Morgan 1994). In recent years, the political representatives of Loyalist political parties such as the Progressive Unionist Party (PUP) have highlighted the often problematic and frequently hostile relationship between the police and working class Protestants (Ellison and Smyth, 2000).

A further friction in the relationship between the Unionist community and the RUC occurred during the handling of controversial Orange parades, particularly the re-routing of Drumcree from 1998 onwards. The Orange Order saw the restraints upon its parades as part of an erosion of the most visible demonstration of its cultural identity (Jarman and Bryan, 1996). During the standoffs between the protesters and the RUC, the police were often subjected to a relentless cycle of intimidation. Ryder (2000) highlighted incidents where individual officers' personal details were made public and threats made against family members. In some cases police officers' homes were attacked, property damaged and several families were forced to relocate. External monitors heavily praised the actions of the RUC over this period but the price it paid was that its traditional affiliation and sentiment of goodwill from the Unionist community was dramatically eroded (Ryder, 2000).

More recently Loyalist disaffection with the State and the police was most demonstrably evident during the Whiterock riots in September 2005 where live ammunition was used in altercations between the security forces and Loyalist paramilitary groups (BBC News, 12.09.05). If the events of the Anglo-Irish Agreement and Drumcree caused significant erosion in relations between Loyalist communities and the police service, then Whiterock was a definite break. Several nights of rioting between members of the Loyalist communities in Belfast and the security forces following the re-routing of an Orange Order parade resulted in a breakdown in community engagement with the police and other criminal justice agencies. Furthermore, Unionist and Loyalist politicians refused to participate in meetings with the police or engage in District Policing Partnership meetings in protest at the actions of the security organisations. Although most sections of the Unionist/Loyalist community have now re-engaged with the police, tensions still remain.

There is a distinct lack of research surrounding the relationship between the Loyalist community and the police. There is a perception within Nationalist communities that historically the agents of law and order sided with the Protestant/Unionist community. However, the evidence clearly shows that there are numerous incidents that highlight the periodic breakdown of engagement between the police and members of the Unionist/Loyalist community.

Sinn Féin and Policing

After initially endorsing the recommendations of the Patten Report, Sinn Féin withdrew its support due to the amendments made in the form of the Police (Northern Ireland) Act 2000. Sinn Féin considered the changes to the accountability mechanisms, specifically the apparently reduced powers of the Policing Board, as unacceptable and their withdrawal was to mark a further seven year absence from the policing structures of Northern Ireland. This period witnessed a number of turbulent events before Sinn Féin finally endorsed the policing structures in Northern Ireland. The 2003 Assembly Elections saw Sinn Féin poll as the largest Nationalist party, and guaranteed the position of Deputy First Minister in any future devolved consociational agreement. There were political set backs at the end of 2004 and beginning of 2005, which threatened to derail the peace-process and see a return to formal direct rule. These included the £26.5 million robbery of the Northern Bank in Belfast in 2004, which the PSNI along with the Independent Monitoring Commission, who were responsible for assessing levels of paramilitary activity for the British and Irish governments, concluded that Republicans were involved in (IMC 4th Report: 2005). Later in January 2005 it was alleged that the IRA were involved in the murder of Robert McCartney in Belfast (Belfast Telegraph, 27.06.08). Although the PSNI stated they did not believe that the IRA command sanctioned the murder, it did not prevent the threatened derailment of the peace-process. Furthermore, this raised the debate around the Sinn Féin position on policing and the rule of law. Sinn Fein came under extreme public and political pressure to finally endorse the PSNI and formal agencies of the criminal justice system (BBC News, 04.03.05)

By late 2005 the climate improved. In September, in response to a declaration by the IRA in July 2005 that its armed campaign was over (BBC News: 28.07.05), the IMC declared they were satisfied that the IRA had put its weapons beyond use (IICD Report: 2005). The IMC's report was followed by a rapid normalisation of the military structures in Northern Ireland, including the disbanding of the Home Service Battalion of the Royal Irish Regiment (formerly the UDR), the removal of a number of army barracks, and a reduction of the army presence in Northern Ireland from 10,500 in 2005 to about 5,000 two years later (BBC News, 12.03.07).

By late 2006 Sinn Féin's position towards policing and justice structures remained the final obstacle to the devolution of powers to the Stormont Assembly. The St Andrews Agreement (November, 2006) was to be the last set of documents to emerge from negotiations involving the local political parties and the two national governments. The proposals aimed to re-establish a devolved executive in Northern Ireland, and at its core was the agreement that the DUP would share power in the executive with Sinn Féin, and that Sinn Féin would give unequivocal support to the PSNI.

Following on from St Andrews, Sinn Féin engaged in a widespread consultation process with its party members. These included internal party meetings, open republican gatherings and six public meetings, which were attended by thousands of people. Some critics of Sinn Féin, however, accused them of packing the meetings to ensure a favourable outcome towards an already pre-determined decision to support the PSNI (Sunday Business Post, 28.01.07). The Sinn Féin decision to endorse the policing structures required a special Ard Fhéis, on the 28 January 2007, where Sinn Féin members gave Sinn Féin's ruling executive the authority to declare its support for the PSNI and the criminal justice system. In the immediate aftermath of the decision to join the policing board, Sinn Féin leader Gerry Adams made an unambiguous statement regarding the nature of their support for the PSNI, stating:

Let me be very clear. If any citizen is the target of crime, whether it be death riders, drug pushers or rape, or attacks on our elderly, if there are crimes against the people, against citizens, Sinn Féin will be encouraging victims and citizens to cooperate with the police. There is no equivocation or qualification on this (Adams, 2007).

Despite Sinn Féin's decision to offer its endorsement of the PSNI, the relationship with the PSNI remains cautious. Sinn Féin considers its key function within the policing structures as being to ensure accountability, establishing policing with the community as the core function of the PSNI, as well as promoting truth and reconciliation programmes, particularly into areas such as collusion.

Re-emergence of a Republican threat to policing

Since Sinn Féin has taken its position within the policing structures there have been those within the Republican movement and wider Republican community who have disagreed with the strategy. In response a number of Republicans have become affiliated with dissident Republican paramilitary groups (Real IRA and the Continuity IRA) and returned to violence and intimidation. By the end of 2007 there had been a marked rise in dissident Republican antagonism, with death threats made against Sinn Féin councillors and DPP members (Sunday Life, 09.12.07). November 2007 saw a peak in the level of violence, with two police officers being shot by dissident Republicans (The Guardian, 13.11.07). However, there is also the view that:

These attacks are not part of any long-term coherent strategy. Barring a truly monumental turn-around in the peace process, they appear to represent the last fluttering of the standard of physical force republicanism (Moran, 2008).

It is important not to over-estimate the level of opposition to the Police Service. The ability to wreak havoc often presents dissidents and fringe organisations with a distorted importance in political matters. Despite this, an undercurrent of Republican opposition to policing structures does exist. Several DPP meetings have been greeted by Republican protests, most notable for the fact that the meetings picketed were after Sinn Féin took their seats on the DPP. This might indicate that the protest was directed at Sinn Féin rather than, as might be assumed, the police (An Phoblacht, 06.12.07). High profile Sinn Féin members have also been heckled at the DPP meetings as traitors (BBC News 20.11.07). Although the motion in favour of taking its positions within the Policing Board was passed by the Ard Fheis with a convincing majority, there is a clear, if marginal, undercurrent in wider Republicanism that Sinn Féin capitulated and betrayed its status as the proponent of an all-Ireland ambition. There appears to be genuine concern that Sinn Féin has effectively forfeited its all-Ireland policies by engaging in the structures of Northern Ireland, and in recognising the legitimacy of the PSNI in Northern Ireland.

Perceptions of the PSNI

Renamed and reformed in 2001, the PSNI has undergone lengthy processes of normalisation in the new post-conflict environment. Structural reforms meant that in April 2002, the first graduates of 50:50 recruitment stepped out, marking the first stage in rectifying the large imbalance between Catholic and Protestant members of the PSNI. The Northern Ireland Policing Board have conducted a number of surveys to determine the levels of public support and engagement for the PSNI. Generally there have been no significant changes in the public's views of the police since 2001. In relation to questions around people's perceptions as to whether they think the police do a good job in Northern Ireland, those that agree from the Catholic community consistently number around 53 per cent. Those from the Protestant community who also agree consistently number around 65 per cent (NIPB Surveys, 2002-2006).

In terms of the broader attitudes, a recent NIPB Survey from May 2007 states that 82 per cent of all respondents are as confident, if not more confident, in the PSNI than they were in 2006. In the same poll, 25 per cent of Catholics indicated that they are more confident in the PSNI than they were during the same period in 2006. This confidence appeared to increase in the immediate aftermath of Sinn Féin's decision to support the PSNI. Sinn Féin's decision to support the PSNI has marked a general improvement in level of support for the PSNI within Catholic communities (Table 1). The period between January-May 2007 witnessed a 6 per cent increase in support for the PSNI compared to the level of support prior to Sinn Féin's decision, from 69 per cent to 75 per cent.

Table 1: Support for the PSNI Pre/Post Sinn Féin decision, 2007

	Catholic	Protestant	Overall
Pre-decision	69%	84%	78%
Post-decision (May 2007)	75%	83%	80%

Source: Northern Ireland Policing Board: Research into Recent Crime Trends in Northern Ireland: May 2007

Although these statistics provide strong evidence for the increased support for the police they have to be met with a degree of caution. Mulcahy (2006) and Ellison (1998) have highlighted the problems associated with using survey data to assess public support for the police.

A recent NISRA Survey (2008) provides a slightly different analysis of current attitudes and perceptions of the police; it concluded that Protestants (78 per cent) had greater overall confidence in policing compared to Catholics (70 per cent). Furthermore, 84 per cent of Protestants believe that the police treat both Catholics and Protestants equally, compared with 63 per cent of Catholic respondents.

Devolution of policing and justice

Since 1972 Westminster has had direct control over law and order in Northern Ireland. However, the St Andrews Agreement (2006) envisaged that if power sharing became a reality then the devolution of policing and justice would occur by 8 May 2008. This date was not met, and as yet policing and justice has not been devolved to the Stormont Assembly. The two dominant political parties, Sinn Féin and the DUP, are in agreement that the departments should be devolved but disagree on when this should take place. Sinn Féin maintains that the time is right and that the devolution of policing and justice is a crucial element of the successful implementation of the St Andrews Agreement. On the other hand the DUP have reserved judgement and have indicated that the public confidence is not there to transfer the powers of policing and justice.

A recent survey conducted by Millward Brown Ulster of over 1,400 people examined their views on the transfer of powers. When asked whether policing and justice should be devolved from Westminster to local politicians a majority of respondents (60 per cent) indicated yes, with 21 per cent replying no and 19 per cent unsure. In relation to the timescale for devolution 53 per cent felt that May 2008 was the correct period for devolution, 21 per cent noted that it was too soon, while a further 9 per cent indicated that it wasn't soon enough (Irish Times, 2008).

The Report on the Inquiry into the Devolution of Policing and Justice Matters (2008), published by a working group established through the Assembly, recognised the sensitive and complex issues associated with the devolution of powers noting *'it has been viewed by some as representing a risk to political developments in Northern Ireland, whereas others have considered that it provides an opportunity to secure political stability'.* Although the committee reached agreement on a number of key issues, the political parties had different views on the timing for devolution, and given the diverse opinions, the committee was unable to reach a general consensus.

Summary

From 1921 to the present day, policing in Northern Ireland has been a divisive and controversial topic, with the two dominant communities, Nationalists/Republicans and Unioinsts/Loyalists, having very different views and experiences of policing. This section has charted chronologically the various events and policing responses that have dominated life in Northern Ireland. The key changes to policing and the numerous pieces of legislation that were introduced to assist the police and security forces combat the paramilitaries have also been documented. It was evident that experiences and perceptions of discrimination, intimidation, and sectarianism had influenced Nationalists/Republicans' opinions of policing. Likewise, the majority of Unionists/Loyalists had positive views of policing, a sense of pride and affiliation with the police and security forces, although it did become apparent that throughout the 1980s and 1990s elements within Loyalism distanced themselves from the police. Post-ceasefires there have been a number of monumental developments in relation to policing with the publication and implementation of the Patten Report recommendations, and the decision from Sinn Fein and Republicans to endorse policing being the most significant. Policing is now operating in a post-conflict society and attempting to develop strategies and policies that incorporate the views and interests of the local communities.

3. Loyalists, Republicans and Community-based Policing

The previous chapter outlined the major developments in policing and the criminal justice system in Northern Ireland since 1921. The following section highlights the role of Loyalist and Republican paramilitaries in the administration of their own methods of 'policing and justice'. Following this will be a documentation of the various community-based programmes that were established in the post-ceasefire years in response to growing incidents of anti-social behaviour and criminality in these working class communities.

Paramilitary policing

Throughout the Troubles paramilitary organisations adopted alternative systems of dealing with and controlling members of their own respective communities and which operated outside of the formal criminal justice system. According to Feenan (2002):

The punishments can range from warnings to violent physical assaults or shootings. They include: warnings, curfews, fines/victim restitution, acts of public humiliation, assaults, shootings, expulsions, assignations, property damage and intimidation.

Republicans and Loyalists adopted very different rationales and justifications for employing policing measures within their respective communities. Central to any validation for the use of alternative forms of criminal justice was the view that Republican paramilitaries had an obligation to protect and serve their community in what they perceived to be the absence of a legitimate police and criminal justice system (Monaghan, 2002). Republican paramilitaries indicated a strong sense of communal responsibility to defend and protect their community, which underpinned their broader military commitments (Cavanaugh, 1997). There was a general perception that the criminal justice system had been slow, costly and lenient with offenders. However, community demand and support for immediate solutions to rising levels of anti-social behaviour are widely regarded by several authoritative observers as the central component in the paramilitaries assuming a justice role within their communities (Sluka 1989; McEvoy and Mika 2002; Winston 1997; Brewer et al 1998).

While there were many from within the community who supported Republican attempts to respond to criminal behaviour, there were also critics. O'Doherty (1998) has refuted claims from Republicans that they were serving the community, and criticised IRA activity as a means of expressing power and control over the community through a form of *'nakedly obvious intimidation'* with moralistic justifications which were gauche and transparent. Kennedy (1995) argued that punishments helped to *'manufacture community support'* against the state, exercised control through terror, and kept IRA volunteers busy while on cease-fire.

While the absence of state legitimacy is perceived to have no relevance amongst Loyalists, successive political developments compromised the legitimacy of the former RUC and the PSNI in the eyes of many Loyalists. Initially at the outbreak of the 'Troubles' Loyalist paramilitary organisations were not intent on challenging the formal policing system, instead they aimed to complement it with their own policing duties that consisted of neighbourhood patrols and street blockades. However the paramilitaries reserved the right to administer their own forms of justice if the criminal justice system did not, in their eyes, adequately deal with offenders (Monaghan, 2002). Gradually there was a breakdown in relationships between the Loyalist community and the police. According to Winston et al (1999) this was in part due to the perceived failure of many statutory agencies to understand local community issues. A strong sense of frustration emerged in regard to the police, with a general perception that they failed to do their job. The frustration extended to the wider criminal justice system, with the courts being perceived as too lenient and paramilitary punishment providing a more tangible, visible and immediate form of retribution (Winston, 1997). In the late 1990s, when paramilitary punishments were common, a research study reinforced this claim with the Northern Ireland Community Crime Survey (O'Mahony et al, 2000) finding that Protestant lower working class urban areas had the highest rate (41.2 per cent) of respondents who did not report incidents to the police because they believed that the police could do nothing.

As noted, there were distinctive differences between the reasons why Loyalists and Republicans administered their forms of 'community justice'. This was further compounded by the fact that Loyalist paramilitaries were structured differently to their Republican counterparts. Unlike Republican paramilitaries there was no specific unit within Loyalist paramilitaries assigned to punishment duties (Bell, 1996). Furthermore, a higher proportion of punishments by Loyalists were 'in-house' in that they involved the internal disciplining of its members (Silke, 1999). Conway (1997) also differentiated between the two and suggested that Loyalists were more involved in policing their own organisations for reasons such as internal disputes and informing whilst Republicans concentrated on policing their areas to garner support for their position within the community.

Following the first ceasefires in 1994 a number of ex-prisoners began a process of examination in an attempt to develop non-violent alternatives to the punishment beatings and shootings. Both Loyalists and Republicans, with the support of academics and statutory organisations, devised models of restorative justice that were unique for their specific communities. The term restorative justice has come to mean different things to different people in Northern Ireland but according to Mika (2006) restorative justice is:

'both a framework and a vision of a just and peaceful society. Restorative justice seeks to both maximise the involvement of all stakeholders – offenders, victims, families, support networks, community representatives, and justice professionals – in the collective tasks of responding to the needs of victims, holding offenders to account, and creating the conditions for reducing and preventing future harms'.

Republican activists began to devise programmes that focused upon restorative justice, human rights, crime prevention, mediation and non-violence, which were exclusive of the police. The 'Blue Book' outlined a model of non-violent and lawful community-based alternatives to punishment beatings and shootings (Auld et al, 1997). In an article published in the Anderstown News (29.04.99) the IRA expressed its support for community-based restorative justice projects as mechanisms for their 'responsible disengagement' from punishment attacks (McEvoy, 2001) and Community Restorative Justice Ireland (CRJI) was established within Republican areas in an attempt to reduce punishment beatings and shootings.

In Loyalist areas research was conducted on the use of punishment attacks by paramilitaries in the Greater Shankill area of West Belfast (Winston, 1997). The research revealed that there was strong support from the Ulster Volunteer Force (UVF) and the Progressive Unionist Party (PUP) to explore viable alternatives to punishment attacks within a certain framework, however in some situations non-violent alternatives would not be accepted as a satisfactory option, i.e. sexual and violent offences, internal paramilitary disputes and drug related matters. From this research Shankill Alternatives emerged, based on the principles of restorative justice and liaising directly with relevant paramilitary groups (McEvoy, 2001). One of the distinctive differences between this restorative justice programme and the one adopted by the Republicans was that Alternatives engaged with the police on a regular basis.

A recent evaluation by Mika (2006) of several restorative justice schemes concluded that they had caused a notable drop in the number of beatings and shootings compared to similar areas that did not have restorative justice programmes in operation. Furthermore, community leaders had indicated that the projects had become essential community assists and had contributed to increasing tolerance for marginalised members of the community, including delinquent youth and former combatants. Two more recent evaluations of these programmes by the Criminal Justice Inspectorate Northern Ireland (2007, 2008) reinforced the positive impact of these initiatives and also noted that both would adhere to a new protocol detailing the arrangements governing community referral of cases of low level criminality to PSNI and the Public Prosecution Service for a determination on their suitability for a community-based disposal as opposed to traditional prosecution through the courts.

Alongside the restorative justice programmes are a number of other community-based initiatives that focused more on crime prevention and addressing concerns around community safety. Throughout the 1990s during the height of the interface violence involving Loyalist and Republican communities, individuals became involved in interface groups and forums to develop relationships and sustain communications to dispel myths and rumours that were frequently attributed as the catalyst for the violence. The majority of these groups did not have a police involvement but were responsible for successfully limiting large incidents of violence and disorder (Jarman and O'Halloran, 2000). A further development was the introduction of Mobile Phone Networks (MPN) in a number of interface communities (Hamilton, 2001). These networks involved the coming together of residents who resided in interface areas. There was a structured format for telephone holders to call on specific times in relation to behaviour on the interface. Essentially the MPNs empowered residents to take responsibility for incidents in their respective areas.

In Republican communities a number of community safety based programmes were developed soon after the cease-fires to support local communities and address concerns around anti-social and criminal behaviour in the Greater Belfast area. Community Watch is a non-violent, community-based approach to issues of criminality. It involves the organised patrols of local residents in specific neighbourhoods who apply co-ordinated and non-violent methods to problems facing their communities. Those associated with these programmes do not perceive themselves as vigilantes, nor have a paramilitary influence, and they are not politically motivated (Irish News, 24.07.08). One example of a Community Watch programme is the Greater St James scheme in West Belfast.

A further community-based initiative developed within Republican areas was the Safer Neighbourhoods Programme. This is a model of community engagement that has empowered the local community to work with statutory bodies and more recently criminal justice organisations in a multi-agency strategy to address issues of criminality, but to also increase community capacity and development. Initially, these organisations had limited or no engagement with the police or other criminal justice agencies. However, since Sinn Féin endorsed the PSNI in January 2008 the forums and the police have begun the process of developing positive working partnerships. One example of these forums is the Upper Springfield Safer Neighbourhood Forum (Belfast Telegraph, 14.05.08) that has significantly contributed to a decrease in incidents of anti-social behaviour and attempted to alleviate the fear of crime in the local area.

Within Loyalist communities there have also been community-based initiatives that have aimed to involve local people taking responsibility for issues that are specific and relevant to their own communities. A number of forums and working groups were initiated to address problems around parading. One example is the North and West Belfast Parades Forum which consists of senior Unionist/Loyalist figures who have attempted to alleviate community tensions around parades, decrease incidents of anti-social behaviour and also take responsibility for the marshalling of parades, thus decreasing the level of time and resources police have to contribute to these events. There are also examples of community initiatives attempting to examine community problems, and also facilitate relationships with the police. The Inner East Forum in East Belfast (Byrne, 2005) consists of community representatives, local business people, statutory representatives and members of the clergy meeting regularly to share information and provide feedback of local initiatives within the area, exploring issues around community safety and relationships between the local community and the police.

Summary

It has been apparent that since the paramilitary ceasefires in 1994 there have been a number of developments within communities in relation to addressing concerns around criminal activity and anti-social behaviour.

Prior to the ceasefires paramilitary organisations controlled and policed their communities with the threat of violent punishment. On occasions these actions were both condemned and supported by members of their communities. However, since the ceasefires Republicans and some Loyalist paramilitaries (UVF, RHC) have endorsed the use of restorative justice techniques to address criminal and anti-social behaviour. On top of this, both communities have developed community-based programmes around community safety to address concerns over the fear of crime and anti-social behaviour. Significantly, a large number of these initiatives whether they are viewed as programmes that reflect 'community justice' or 'community policing' have been established with minimal or no input from the police. The question now is how compatible these community-based programmes are with those that exist within the context of the criminal justice system? The following chapters will attempt to address this point, and highlight further key themes from discussions with the main protagonists in the policing debate.

4. Nationalist/Republican Views

A number of discussions were held with Nationalist and Republican community representatives along with individuals involved with local community safety initiatives. Furthermore, local residents from Republican communities participated in several informal interviews. Upon reflection there were three types of Republicans interviewed for this research. There were those who supported Sinn Féin in their decision to endorse the PSNI. There were others who were more critical of Sinn Féin and had ceased to support them but continued to advocate a Republican ideology. Finally, there were individuals who agreed with the policy of violence shown by dissident Republicans. Discussions centred on their perceptions, issues and concerns around policing and the PSNI. Specific focus was also placed on existing community safety mechanisms and their future relationship within the formal criminal justice system. A number of themes emerged from these discussions and have been outlined below.

The policing legacy

The most significant area of discussion centred on the historical aspects of policing. All of those interviewed had negative experiences of policing and maintained they were discriminated against as a result of their community background. Furthermore, they were harassed physically and verbally and generally perceived that they were treated very differently to those from a Unionist/Loyalist background. The interviewees felt that their past perceptions and experiences of policing reflected the majority of those from the Republican community:

The majority of them (police) would have seen West Belfast as a reservation to contain the natives, and people could do what they wanted as long as it was kept internal (Community worker).

Interviewees claimed that there was no past association or relationship with the police. The Nationalist/Republican communities found it difficult to identity with the criminal justice system. The police were seen as a military force supporting the Unionist community with the assistance of the British Army:

They were police stations in England and Scotland, here they were police barracks…we grew up and they weren't from our community, they were seen as a Protestant force, as a force for the state…you just accepted it (Mainstream Republican).

A number of respondents recounted incidents where they and members of their family had been treated in an abusive and discriminatory manner by the security forces. These memories were relatively fresh and to a degree influenced their perceptions and views of the police in a contemporary context:

Our community was coming under attack from Loyalists yet the police pointed their guns at us (Critical Republican).

The impact of the conflict and the position of policing within that environment could not be understated. It was the single most significant factor inhibiting the relationship between the community and the police in the current climate. There were also reservations around how far individual officers had embraced the changes in policing, several respondents felt that the experiences of officers who served throughout the conflict would impact on their ability to work in partnership with the Republican community in this new dispensation for law and order:

We were at war with them and they were at war with us. If you had someone belonging to you attacked by a rocket you are hardly going to be predisposed to police that community (Mainstream Republican).

The history of policing from a Nationalist/Republican perspective has long been a contentious issue. Throughout the conflict policing from the community's view has focused on counter-insurgency policies and therefore distanced itself from delivering a fair and inclusive policing service. Furthermore, the nature of the conflict restricted the community's opportunities to access and utilise the resources of the police.

Transition period

According to interviewees there had been a degree of unease within the Republican community in relation to community safety in the period since the paramilitaries had wound down and the endorsement of the PSNI. Throughout the conflict recorded incidents of crime and anti-social behaviour were relatively low within staunch Republican communities. There was an acknowledgement that many within the Republican community had disagreed with paramilitary policing and recognised that it had not been successful in reducing crime. However, for many there was a sense of reassurance with the knowledge that there was a mechanism that could, if needed, address one's immediate concerns in a quick and visible manner:

In the past they could always rely on the IRA…if they had a particular problem they could go down to one of the centres and get it taken care of. They had a safety blanket, they might not have needed it, but at least it was there (Mainstream Republican).

Furthermore, for over thirty years it had been instilled into the local communities by Sinn Féin and the IRA that there was to be no engagement or fraternisation with agencies in the criminal justice system. Therefore, communities had limited or no experience of working with the police. For many reporting crime to the police was an entirely new concept. Respondents recognised the need for the PSNI, and welcomed Sinn Féin's and the Republican movement's endorsement of the criminal justice system. Between the paramilitary ceasefires and the developments with the PSNI there had been a lot of pressure placed on community workers in the Republican communities:

There was a practical need for a police service…we couldn't deal with the crime. When I was in the IRA you walked up to a bunch of kids and they listened to you…now when you walk up to them, they tell you to fuck off and it's a free country (Former IRA member).

It was important to note that a number of respondents acknowledged a hesitancy in using the PSNI. There was a realisation that there was a broad endorsement from the Republican movement of the PSNI but there continued to be a difficulty in differentiating the PSNI from the RUC:

Patten hasn't really been implemented…there have been some cosmetic changes, obviously the name and badge, but on the ground we haven't noticed any change in their attitude (Critical Republican).

It was evident that there was a degree of uncertainty within Republican communities around the delivery of policing and responding to issues of crime, anti-social behaviour and community safety. There was a policing vacuum between the ceasefires and the Republican endorsement of the PSNI. The paramilitaries were not engaged in 'house-keeping' duties, yet the Republican movement had not endorsed the police. This was an uncertain time for communities, which according to several respondents saw a steady rise in criminal behaviour and an increase in the fear of crime.

Community support

There were two key areas of discussion that focused on the levels of support for Republican communities in developing relationships and engaging with the PSNI in early 2007. These centred on the role of Sinn Féin at a political level and the wider Republican movement at the grass roots level. There was general agreement that at a strategic level Sinn Féin had canvassed public opinion, debated the rationale for endorsing the formal policing structures, and taken an inevitable decision within the context of the peace process. However, there were also a number of interviewees who felt that although Sinn Féin had endorsed the PSNI at a strategic and political level, they had failed to provide local communities with the support in their practical engagements with the PSNI. The majority of people had no previous experience of engaging positively with the police. It was a new experience and one that many found extremely difficult:

I think that Sinn Féin done the political deal on policing and that was fine at that level. However, I think that made absolutely no difference on the street corner to kids or people who have a long memory of what the cops done on them as teenagers (Critical Republican).

Several respondents recalled the immediate days after the decision was made on the 28th January 2007 to endorse the PSNI. According to many it was a period of uncertainty and confusion. Local communities were unsure of the procedures, a large number did not believe that the decision had been taken to participate and engage with the formal policing structures. One respondent maintained that there was no direction for local people, or information on how to simply interact with the PSNI:

On the Monday morning people did not have a clue what to do...Sinn Féin did not know how to facilitate relationships between the community and the police. There was no direction or leadership. It was left up to local community safety groups to take the lead (Community worker).

However, there were those that maintained that Sinn Féin led from the front and supported communities in adapting to the new social environment where police engagement was to be welcomed. There was an acknowledgement of the difficulties people had in accepting the police, but Sinn Féin were viewed as a key mechanism in breaking down the barriers:

For a lot of people policing is a raw issue. They have no confidence in the police and are reluctant to engage with them, they have had a lifetime of saying no. However, Sinn Féin have shown strong leadership. They have condemned attacks against the police and encouraged people to use them and report crime (Mainstream Republican).

A further illustration of the Republican movement's commitment to policing was evident when the central Republican paramilitary organisation, the IRA, publicly stated that it would not return to its past practice of delivering informal justice: *'IRA will not police streets'* (Andersonstown News 12.04.08). There had been a steady rise in incidents of crime in local Republican areas with some members of the community calling for the IRA to re-engage in paramilitary policing because the formal system was inadequate.

There is no denying the complex issues that were prevalent within Republican communities in the aftermath of Sinn Féin's decision to endorse policing in Northern Ireland. At a number of practical and emotional levels local communities had to deal with the sensitive issues that quickly emerged. There has been a general consensus that politically Republicanism quickly came to terms with the decision. However, at a community level this acceptance has taken longer to bed down.

Existing Community Programmes

It soon became apparent that pre-existing community safety programmes and restorative justice programmes, namely Safer Neighbourhood Partnerships and Community Restorative Justice Ireland, had performed two key functions since Sinn Féin had endorsed policing. Firstly, they had continued in their role of providing their local communities with programmes around safety, crime and addressing concerns on anti-social behaviour. These organisations were in the unique position of knowing the local areas and the individuals/groups with the potential to engage in anti-social and criminal behaviour:

In a sense nobody knows these communities better than we do, we can identify troublemakers and prevent incidents before they start (Community worker).

A secondary role emerged for these groups soon after Sinn Féin endorsed the PSNI. They inadvertently became a facilitator or a type of conduit between the local communities and the PSNI:

They are coming to us and they are looking for us to go with them to provide them with the notion of acceptability, respectability and the idea that it is OK to go to the cops (CRJI representative).

According to respondents this role of 'broker' was completely unexpected but necessary. There was so much confusion at the beginning and communities felt that existing programmes had the skills, capacity, and knowledge to support them in those first months of uncertainty around engagement with the various agencies of the criminal justice system:

For forty years people were told if they went to the peelers they would be executed or put out of the country, but now all of a sudden we are saying that they are the only people who are eligible or capable of ensuring law and order...its bound to be confusing (Mainstream Republican).

Discussions also examined respondents' views on the compatibility of local community safety and restorative justice programmes and initiatives within the formal criminal justice system. There was an acknowledgement from several interviewees that the police alone could not be solely responsible for addressing the community's concerns around crime and anti-social behaviour:

The cops can't do everything. There needs to be a joined up approach and the community needs to be at the heart of it (Community worker).

Existing community programmes were viewed as the key for this partnership approach. The onus was on the formal criminal justice system to embrace the community initiatives and attempt to both utilise and incorporate the knowledge base and experience, and combine this with the resources and capacity of the police to address areas of criminality:

If you get one more police officer into our community you're getting an extra pair of eyes...but if you go into partnership with the existing community safety group you are getting an entire community (Mainstream Republican).

One other issue to bear in mind relates to the level of community involvement in programmes associated with the police and other agencies in the criminal justice system. According to respondents members of the police do not reside in working class Republican or Loyalist communities, therefore they are detached from individuals and specific incidents. However, those from the community who engage proactively with the police, participate in community safety initiatives and promote closer working partnerships with the police are putting themselves at risk:

Several of the hoods (young people engaged in anti-social behaviour) see us from the community as part of the policing apparatus. This is very dangerous...the police don't live here, we do (Community worker).

Community engagement with the PSNI has been a slow but successful process. Local communities have looked for support and encouragement in contacting the PSNI. Much of this has come from existing community safety and restorative justice programmes. They have been in the unique position to provide leadership and instil the confidence in working with all of the agencies in the criminal justice system.

Community expectations

There is a clear and unequivocal demand for policing from the majority of people in Northern Ireland. Republican communities are engaging positively with the police on a number of levels. The communities have invited the police onto local community safety partnerships, and the police have begun to attend community events. However, the question has to be asked as to whether Republican communities feel that the PSNI are responding in kind. According to respondents there is an unprecedented level of expectancy within local communities around addressing crime and community safety issues:

One of the main questions now is around the effectiveness of the PSNI but I think coupled with that is the expectation of the Nationalist population about what they should and can expect from a police service (CRJI representative).

In the past issues and concerns around policing centred on the legitimacy of the police, now they are focused firmly on the delivery of service. For the most part, Republican communities have limited or no experience of working with the police or other criminal justice organisations. It is a new concept for them. Therefore, several respondents maintained that the community's expectations of policing would outweigh the realities of policing:

I do believe that the expectations of the Nationalist/Republican community are too high in terms of what to expect from policing, but I think that's because they don't know any better, they have never had the experience of policing (Critical Republican).

The media and television programmes such as *The Bill* and *CSI* have shaped many people's perceptions around policing and justice. The realities of policing are very different. The PSNI have issues around resources and capacity. The formal criminal justice system is more cumbersome and slower to dispense justice that communities expect. Prioritisation is a new concept for communities. During the conflict there was a highly visible police presence. Security dominated people's lives in which they regularly encountered police and army on the streets. This is no longer the case, yet the perception still exists that the police have an unlimited budget and can respond to every query.

In relation to service delivery there was an expectation that the police would have a visible presence within the communities, that they would be walking the streets, or on bicycles in high visibility jackets. The community wanted to know that if they reported crime then the police would respond positively, provide information and keep them informed of all developments. The key element in regards to service delivery related to arrests and prosecutions. Perceptions of safety were affected by the ability of the police to arrest and detain offenders. It was imperative that the police were seen to be responding appropriately to criminal behaviour as this reflected upon how the community viewed the police.

Respondents were asked whether there was an appetite within communities for a return to the informal justice techniques employed by the paramilitaries. There was an acknowledgement that if the community's expectations were not met in relation to community safety and the fear of crime then there was the potential for people to remonstrate for their return. However, it was generally accepted that paramilitary violence did not work:

There is a nostalgia, almost like the good old days when the IRA shot them, the IRA broke their legs, when the IRA put them out of the country...but it never worked. The IRA couldn't solve the problem and people realise that (Community representative).

It was interesting to note that community concerns on policing centred on service delivery and not the legitimacy of the organisation. The Republican community appeared willing to engage with the PSNI, but concerns were evident as to whether this expectant community understood the realities of policing.

Criminal activity

Discussions then turned to whether respondents felt there was more crime and anti-social behaviour in their communities than in previous years. According to the PSNI recorded crime throughout Northern Ireland dropped by 10.5 per cent from 2006/07 to 2007/08 (PSNI, 2008). However, respondents perceived a growing crime problem within their communities, and felt that violent crime was a particular problem in working class areas. There was a consensus from interviewees that this emerged soon after the paramilitary ceasefires in the 1990s:

In the early days when I grew up criminals in the area just knew their place, we didn't have crime. It's when the war ended that it all started (Critical Republican).

There appeared to be a policing vacuum between the ending of the conflict and the Agreement in 1998 and Sinn Féin endorsing policing in early 2007:

During the peace process the Provies (IRA) couldn't do anything, yet the police weren't welcome either. That has added to the whole anti-social problem round here, for long periods there was nothing (Mainstream Republican).

Local media picked up on this fear of crime and anti-social behaviour. To a large extent youths were seen as responsible for the perceived increase in violence and crime: *'Local teens turn Falls area into Beirut'* (Irish News 19.11.07). This headline referred to the steady increase in criminal and anti-social behaviour from a collection of young people from the Republican Falls community.

The issues and concerns raised in the discussions were not viewed as simply originating in Republican communities. Interviewees maintained that crime involving young people was prevalent throughout working class areas in Northern Ireland and beyond. There was agreement that in post-conflict society, communities were experiencing 'normal crime' for the first time:

There is an increasing drug problem, you have active and organised hoods…these groups feel more cocky and arrogant without the threat of the IRA or other paramilitaries, we are seeing problems that are experienced in major cities throughout Ireland (Community worker).

It was interesting to note that several respondents referred to the lack of respect young people had for authority figures within their local communities. There was no difference in their views of the police or well-known local individuals prominent within the Republican movement:

You know young people today are acting towards adults in this community and people linked to the Ra (IRA) in the same way we used to view the RUC…total disgust. There is no respect for authority figures regardless of who they are (Mainstream Republican).

All of the respondents perceived that there had been an increase in crime in the last few years. They maintained that there had been a serious decline in the behaviour of young people, and acknowledged that the time between the ceasefires and Sinn Féin's endorsement of the police had created a vacuum where young people had engaged in illegal activities within an environment which had limited success in curtailing their behaviour.

Police response

There was a general indication that the PSNI had engaged in a number of activities and initiatives at a strategic and political level with the emphasis on instilling a sense of community confidence in the police, and developing meaningful partnerships and levels of engagement. They had participated in a District Policing Partnership (DPP) meeting in West Belfast, organised public meetings and workshops with community workers to develop complementary community safety strategies, and participated in a number of youth led initiatives which highlighted the impact of violent crime on the wider community. However, a number of respondents had received complaints from members of their community in relation to the conduct of particular police officers and the quality of service. There were issues around the behaviour of officers, but more importantly the lack of information given to those who have reported a crime:

There have been complaints that the police response has not been satisfactory, they don't phone back, slow to respond, don't show any courtesy and basically don't want to know (Community worker).

There was a realisation that the police did not have the resources to deal with everything that was being asked of them. Local communities were anxious and apprehensive about the extent to which the police could meet their expectations and facilitate an environment in which the community's concerns around crime were alleviated:

I think that there is a level of unease in the community and a lack of faith in the ability of the PSNI to keep people safe (Mainstream Republican).

Discussions then centred on the realities of community policing, and what the local community actually felt it entailed. There were two emerging themes based on the experiences of respondents highlighting the terminology and language used, along with the techniques employed while operating in a community environment. Firstly, a number of respondents complained that policing was becoming more about targets, figures and statistics. The personal contact and individuality of policing was diminishing. The police constantly talked about visible policing and developing relationships and addressing local concerns. However, the reality was more about clearance rates, policing jargon and graphs, which was actually introducing a barrier between the community and the police:

They are talking to you in statistics, saying there has been a percentage point increase or decrease, but what does that mean? This doesn't answer people's fears on the ground (Community worker).

The second theme related to the methods of engagement on different occasions between the police and local communities. A number of respondents felt that elements within the PSNI simply *'did not do community policing'*, especially when dealing with young people:

If you have 30 or 40 youths out drinking the community policing team will go over and engage with them...but the response team will sit in their jeeps and hope they go away (Community worker).

The community distinguished between the attitudes and responses of the various units and sectors within the PSNI. Neighbourhood teams appeared to engage very differently with the community compared to the response teams. Interviewees associated with locally based community safety initiatives advocated an approach around dialogue and confidence building when dealing with young people. However, respondents had experience of police tactics being more aggressive and disengaging when an alternative method may have been appropriate:

They are not on the same wavelength as us in terms of community policing...they still use the TSGs, (Tactical Support Group) the boys in boiler suits, cracking heads and taking drink off kids. Then they pull out and we the community are left to deal with the fallout. We mistakenly thought the cops had the answers to community policing, when the reality is they don't (Community worker).

It was interesting to note that a recent evaluation from Include Youth (2008) that examined a programme aimed at developing relationships between young people and the police in North Belfast concluded that police tactics could have a negative impact on sustaining and building informal and formal partnerships and relationships with teenagers.

It was evident from the discussions that respondents felt that the police had a realistic opportunity to develop meaningful working partnerships with local communities. However, there was a degree of caution from interviewees who noted that it was important that the police responded in a positive manner during their initial contacts with groups. Sinn Féin and prominent Republican community representatives have encouraged people to use and engage with the PSNI. They have endorsed the formal criminal justice system and indicated that this system is the most appropriate method for delivering justice and delivering on issues and concerns around crime and community safety. If the police do not deliver or provide a service that doesn't meet the minimum of a community's expectations then those same people/groups who promote and advocate the PSNI are in a precarious position:

The PSNI are in a make or break situation because if we (community reps) lose credibility in the area because we encouraged people to use the police but the police failed to respond appropriately then the partnerships will collapse (Community worker).

One respondent was hesitant about ongoing levels of engagement between the police and the local community. They felt that they were being judged in the same capacity as the police, yet they had no control over police responses or the behaviour of individual officers:

I feel sometimes that we are on trial and the community need to visibly see a difference or else the PSNI will lose credibility, Sinn Féin will lose credibility and so will the residents associations and community groups who are encouraging people to use the police (Community worker).

According to respondents the police response to call-outs in Republican communities is not at an adequate level. There are concerns around the flow of information and response times. There is a realisation that police resources are not at a level seen during the conflict, and that prioritisation of incidents is a growing necessity. However, these initial contacts will form the basis of a community's views and perceptions of the police.

Developing relationships

The building of relationships has taken place at the strategic/political level and the more operational/grass roots level. There have been a number of symbolic events that have provided the Republican communities with direction and leadership. Sinn Féin have taken their seats on the NIPB, and the Chief Constable has participated in public and private meetings on issues around crime and community safety in Republican West Belfast (Andersonstown News 11.02.08). Prominent community representatives have also participated in discussions with senior police officers, establishing protocols and developing working relationships. These have been sensitive, emotive and on occasions highly charged discussions, but they have established a platform where both Republicans and the police can set out the practical implications of policing in a post-conflict society:

I was fortunate to be part of a group who met with a number of police commanders...we showed them a DVD highlighting a number of incidents from 1921 to the present day including internment and the hunger strikes. I think it was uncomfortable for a lot of them, there was heated debates...but it set out our views on policing and vice versa, it was good for the long term (Republican).

On the ground there was a strong view that more dialogue was needed to instil confidence in the police and criminal justice system. The community needed to hear from the police about the different programmes and techniques that they were developing to address issues of criminality. It was also important to develop these relationships in such a manner that engaging with the police became a normal activity. Several people indicated that the onus of responsibility was on the police to provide the opportunities for engagement. There was some criticism of the police using outside organisations to assess community opinion, instead of them directly engaging with local groups. One interviewee felt that the NIPB surveys and consultations were a barrier between the local community and the PSNI:

We need real genuine dialogue. The PSNI need to be more proactive and get out there and talk to communities instead of having consultants out there doing it for them (Mainstream Republican).

One further criticism related to the constant shift in personnel within the PSNI. A number of respondents had experience of developing positive working partnerships with specific officers within the one geographical area. These relationships had instilled a degree of community confidence in the actual process of policing and contributed to the development of joined up community safety initiatives. However, in a number of cases officers simply moved sectors, units or District Command Units and new officers were introduced in their place:

If we are selling something to someone then its important we know what we are selling. Some of this is personality based, if they keep moving then we don't really know them and then we have to start all over again (Mainstream Republican).

Over the years there have been a number of structures established to assist the police in forging links within communities. However, schemes such as Neighbourhood Watch, Community Safety Forums, and Community Police Liaison Committees (CPLC) were viewed negatively from the perspective of respondents from working class Republican areas. They were often seen as middle class talking shops dealing with issues around noise and traffic concerns, not somewhere that issues facing interface communities could be discussed:

Once we attended one of the community police liaison committees...Jesus, it was like the Vicar of Dibley and the parish council. It was like a time warp...all pensioners whose biggest concerns were around loud engines...in the same period we had three sex attacks and two shootings (Community worker).

It became apparent that community background wasn't actually viewed as a significant factor in the lack of engagement with these groups. Respondents noted that class was a more inhibitive factor in creating the environment where working class people had an opportunity to raise their issues and concerns. The majority of attendees at the CPLC's were from middle and upper class communities with no real perspective of the issues prevalent within working class Republican areas.

Respondents were asked whether DPPs were an opportunity for developing and strengthening the relationship between the police and local communities. There was an acknowledgement that past Sinn Féin and Republican disengagement with these structures had impacted on their ability to fulfil their roles and responsibilities. However, since Sinn Féin had endorsed all of the policing structures there was anticipation that DPPs would form the foundation for strategic thinking involving the community, elected representatives and the police:

DPPs never worked in their previous life, now they have a chance with the full support, participation and endorsement of Sinn Féin and the Republican community (Mainstream Republican).

It was interesting to note that since Sinn Féin had established themselves on the DPPs local communities had noted a significant increase in levels of engagement with the police. Sinn Féin were raising local concerns, challenging the police on response times and generally assisting in creating the confidence where members of the community feel safe accessing and using the police.

Public Prosecution Service and Judiciary

There were a number of criticisms raised in relation to the Public Prosecution Service (PPS) and the courts with respect to the prosecution and sentencing of offenders. A number of respondents were unsure of the working of the PPS and indicated that this was a reflection of the views of the wider Republican community. The central criticism revolved around the length of sentences given to offenders:

The whole judiciary system is a shambles...a juvenile will almost have to commit murder before they are landed with a sentence (Community worker).

Recently communities, through the support of the PSNI, were beginning to gain a more comprehensive understanding of the workings of the PPS. In the past communities assumed that it was the responsibility of the police to prosecute offenders. There was a lack of knowledge about the system, and the police were perceived as encompassing the criminal justice system. However, local communities were beginning to realise that the police were entirely independent of the PPS, and had no responsibility for whether individuals were prosecuted. Communities found it difficult to identify with the PPS, and were not aware of mechanisms open to them to challenge their decisions:

The PPS are cocooned in a wee bubble away from reality...in a wee world of their own with no conception of the issues in working class communities (Mainstream Republican).

Several respondents also felt that the image of the PPS and the apathy from the community towards it had the potential to damage the long-term success of the criminal justice system:

They are the Achilles heel of the criminal justice system...no matter how much accountability or transparency you introduce on the police, the PPS and courts can bring the whole lot down (Mainstream Republican).

The lack of information or explanations around decision-making did little to provide public confidence in the PPS or the judiciary. In fact their actions on occasions could impact on the relationships between the police and local communities.

Dissident threats

Sinn Féin's decision to endorse policing was not welcomed by the entire

Republican movement. There were a number of individuals associated with the party, along with lifetime Republicans, who distanced themselves from the decision:

It was very difficult for some Republicans to accept, it's created a lot of problems. A number of people have resigned from the movement (Critical Republican).

Those that have not supported Sinn Féin's decision on policing can be split into two distinct categories. Firstly, there are those who have left the party and the Republican movement and refuse to endorse or engage with any of the criminal justice agencies. Secondly, there are those who joined dissident Republican paramilitary groups and advocate the use of violence against members of the PSNI. The latter group refuse to accept the PSNI because of what it represents ideologically. They view the PSNI as an acceptance of Westminister and the partition of Ireland, which go against their Republican beliefs.

The PSNI is a sectarian, bigoted organisation that upholds the laws of the British state (Critical Republican).

They refuse to participate with the policing structures and when the opportunity arises engage in protests and demonstrations:

I believe Sinn Féin would have been better outside, protesting and putting pressure on the organisation rather than thinking they could exert change from within (Critical Republican).

The dissident threat is more prevalent and a number of attacks have resulted in injuries to several police officers. Discussions with Republicans revealed that the Real and Continuity IRA were attempting to offer support to communities who were suffering from increased anti-social behaviour and youth crime. Where there was a perceived vacuum in criminal justice structures these groups were offering to *'deal with alleged perpetrators'* in a quick and visible manner. However, there appeared to be no support for these groups in staunch Republican areas. They did not appear to have a coherent strategy and were largely viewed as a collection of thugs and hoods:

They are not a viable threat. They have no popular support within the community…people are tired of the violence. They have seen the big changes in the last few years. They will never have the popular support, but you don't need that if you're going to walk up and shoot a policeman (Critical Republican).

There was a realisation that they could not offer an alternative to the formal criminal justice system. However, it was also stated that these groups had the potential to impact on the types of policing experienced by communities. While there was a continued threat against the police, the police may be reluctant to fully embrace a partnership approach with Republican communities.

Devolution of policing and justice

Considering that devolution of policing was one of the key elements of the St Andrews Agreement (2006), which ultimately led to the restoration of power sharing, it was expected that this topic would dominate discussions. Interestingly, this was not the case, with really only those respondents from a strategic and/or political background offering an analysis:

To the average person the devolution of policing would not be in their top ten issues, but the practical implications are that we need it implemented (Mainstream Republican).

For the majority of people their central concerns focus on addressing crime and the fear of crime. The mechanics behind the delivery of policing are unimportant as long as policing is visible, productive and fulfils its roles and responsibilities. On the other hand, elected representatives and those within the Republican movement recognise both the practical and symbolic importance of having policing and justice powers devolved to the local Assembly:

It was a key tenet of the Agreement, it was supposed to be devolved but certain individuals are now playing politics with policing and justice (Critical Republican).

There was a degree of concern that the devolution of policing and justice powers would become a political issue, and therefore inevitably result in further political talks and negotiations between Sinn Féin, the DUP and British and Irish Governments. However, there appeared to be minimal concern within communities as to who was responsible for administering and overseeing the department.

Summary

The legacy of policing through the conflict remains a sensitive and emotive issue for large sections of the Nationalist/Republican community. The majority of Nationalists and Republicans had limited experiences of policing, and that was usually confrontational. These communities were unable to identify with the policing and criminal justice system in a positive manner. However, there was an acknowledgement that in the ten years since the signing of the Agreement society both required and deserved a modern and professional police service. The role of existing community safety and restorative justice programmes in supporting communities since Sinn Féin's endorsement of the PSNI cannot be understated. They have played a significant part in providing leadership and advice at the grass roots level by encouraging people to use the police and where appropriate facilitating engagement between the community and police.

Issues and complaints around the police now appeared to focus on response times, the flow of information and a lack of visible policing. There was an expectation that the police would deliver and address all of the community's concerns over community safety and criminality. However, the realities of policing are very different. There is a slow realisation within some quarters that the police cannot resolve all of the issues, that a partnership approach is required, and that the community is central to this. The difficulty facing both the PSNI and local communities is how this partnership approach will operate in practice and determining the boundaries between the community taking a responsibility for policing and the PSNI fulfilling their roles and responsibilities.

The decision from Sinn Féin to endorse the PSNI has been welcomed by the majority of the Republican community. However, a number of individuals have left Sinn Fein and been vocal in their criticism of the party. They hold the view that Sinn Féin has abandoned the principles of Republicanism and provided a degree of legitimacy for the Northern Ireland state. Furthermore, there is a small minority who have become affiliated to dissident Republican paramilitary groups who continue to advocate a military approach to the British presence in Northern Ireland. They have also threatened Republicans who endorse the current Sinn Féin strategy and members of the PSNI, but they have not had any significant impact on the development of engagement between Nationalist/Republican communities and the police.

5. Unionist/Loyalist Views

A number of discussions were held with Unionist and Loyalist community representatives along with individuals involved with local community safety initiatives. Furthermore, local residents from Loyalist communities participated in several informal interviews. Discussions centred on their perceptions, issues and concerns around policing and the PSNI. Specific focus was also placed on existing community safety mechanisms and their future relationship within the formal criminal justice system. A number of themes have emerged from these discussions that have been outlined below.

Policing the Conflict

From a Nationalist perspective there has been a widely held view that policing and security organisations garnered more support and recognition in Unionist/Loyalist areas than in Nationalist/Republican communities. According to respondents, the RUC and security forces were held in high esteem throughout the conflict. One respondent felt that a key aspect of policing throughout the conflict was the level of respect for the RUC from the Unionist/Loyalist communities. They were viewed as upholding the rule of law, combating terrorism and protectors of their communities. This meant that regardless of police behaviour or actions they were always viewed in both a sympathetic and respectful manner:

There was this overwhelming support for the police even if they were seen to be a little heavy handed with people…because the next day you would be watching another funeral of a police officer on the television (Unionist).

Unlike today where people feel comfortable criticising the police and complaining about response times and police behaviour, in the past this wasn't the case. The nature of the conflict meant that the RUC were on the front line and subsequently suffered significant numbers of casualties. In a sense it was viewed as almost unpatriotic to pass a negative judgement on the actions of the police:

You didn't criticise, they were our police doing their job in a terrible environment (Unionist).

There is a strongly held view that the legacy of the police during the conflict from a Unionist/Loyalist perspective was one of admiration and bravery. It had a profound effect on how they viewed the police and engaged with them. However, as will become apparent, this was not a view held by all Unionists/Loyalists.

Levels of engagement

It was important to determine the levels of support for the PSNI within Unionist/Loyalist working class communities. It quickly became apparent from several respondents that there had been a significant breakdown in engagement between a number of these communities and the police:

I think that there is a social separation that has happened as a result of the Troubles that has divided Loyalist working class communities and the police (Loyalist).

There had been a distancing in relations with some debate as to when this originated. There were those that felt events such as the Anglo Irish Agreement (1985) or the policing of parades, namely Drumcree in the late 1990s or Whiterock in 2005, were the catalyst for disengagement with the police. However, others were of the opinion that Loyalist working class disengagement with the police began soon after the onset of the Troubles:

There was never this rosy period. Before the Troubles the police were integrated into the working class communities, they lived and socialised there. However, when the Troubles started the police were seen as outsiders, they arrested Loyalist paramilitaries. They no longer could live in the working class communities (Loyalist).

Members of these communities found it difficult to resonate or identify with the police. There was a clear perception that the PSNI could not identify with the issues and concerns that were prevalent within working class communities as they did not reside within them. What has compounded the feeling of isolation and disengagement is that there is a long held view that the police used to be part of the community. There was a romantic attachment to the idea that the police came from the same social and economic background as contemporary Loyalist communities. In a sense they were supposed to have an affiliation with the community they now policed, but the reality was that the majority of police had no attachment with the areas they operated in. The irony of Loyalist disengagement with police was not lost on a number of respondents:

There has been a great effort put into developing engagement with the Republican community...but the Loyalist community has been largely ignored to the extent where they feel totally disengaged with the police (Loyalist).

It was evident that relationships between the police and Loyalist working class communities had fragmented in recent years. To some extent there appeared to be a chasm growing between Loyalist communities and the police that did not exist thirty years ago. Political events along with the policing of parades have compounded this sense of community alienation with the PSNI which for many has been ignored at a political level with the continued focus on Republican communities.

Patten recommendations

Discussions then focused on the impact of the Patten Report and the subsequent changes to the RUC. It was important to determine whether the significant changes in policing had altered their views on the organisation. According to respondents it was a very sensitive and emotive issue within large sections of the Unionist/Loyalist communities. Changes to the name, uniform and symbols were seen as unnecessary and disrespectful to the memory of those serving officers who had been killed during the conflict. One of the most contentious issues centred on the recruitment for the PSNI which was based on a policy of 50 per cent of all trainee intake being from the Catholic community, in order to address the under-representation of Catholics within the police service:

How many people from Loyalist working class areas are in the police? The 50:50 means it is near impossible for them to join the service (Community worker).

One result of this policy was that the PSNI were not viewed as reflecting the communities that they policed. Respondents were unable to identify any new recruits from Loyalist working class areas in which they had resided. They were aware of many who had applied but all were unsuccessful:

I was in the RUC...my daughter has applied four times and hasn't got in. Apparently she is from the wrong ethnic group. She went to England and is now a serving officer over there (Unionist).

It was interesting to note a significant impact of this policy was that young people from Loyalist areas were finding it more and more difficult to relate and identify with the police. There was a growing chasm between the police and this sub section of the community.

Not all of the respondents were critical of the Patten recommendations. There was a realisation that there had to be a change so that the entire community could both identify and embrace policing:

It was a time for change and this had to be embraced by both Loyalists and Republicans, without their support it would not have worked (Loyalist).

Within the context of Unionist/Loyalist history there has been a strong affiliation and association with the police. Whether this was a reality or more a blurring of perceptions is open to interpretation. However, what is not in question was the criticism and hostility shown towards the Patten report and the subsequent implementation of its recommendations.

Experiences of policing

The majority of respondents were quite negative in their comments about their experiences of policing. There was a general perception that the police were unconcerned with the issues in Loyalist working class communities:

Round here the PSNI stands for Police Service No Interest (Loyalist)

A number of respondents recalled their experiences with the police, and for the most part this was not very positive. General complaints focused on the delivery of the service, with specific attention placed on communication and the sharing of information:

What is the point in ringing the police? First of all you aren't sure who you are speaking to, most times you get re-routed to central control. Then you get an officer who doesn't know the area. Then if they do come out they are not desperately interested, they pass on their notes to the local officers. They, if you're lucky, get in touch a week later, though most time you never hear from them again (Unionist).

According to interviewees these experiences were reflective of many from within working class Unionist/Loyalist communities. Furthermore, there was a sense of frustration from those who were encouraging local people to contact the PSNI and they were subsequently not receiving an adequate service. Potentially, there was a risk of people deciding not to report crime to the PSNI. Issues around the delivery of a policing service were placed within the context of decreased resources for the PSNI. There was an acknowledgement that there were fewer police officers than before, and this in turn fostered a belief that the PSNI would not respond to all call-outs:

We don't think that policing has improved. In fact we think the opposite has happened. They no longer have the officers (Unionist).

During the discussions it became apparent that a large number of respondents had not experienced meeting the PSNI in a situation that did not require a policing response. Their first experiences usually meant they were a victim or perpetrator of an alleged crime. They were not used to engaging with the police in a normal environment such as a community festival or a meeting:

The majority of policing we see is reactionary, it is too aggressive…they don't want to see us in normal circumstances (Community worker).

A community's first experience of policing will more often than not dictate their levels of co-operation and engagement on future issues of crime and community safety. According to respondents, Loyalist working class communities have very negative experiences of policing in relation to response times and the sharing of information. This potentially could influence their roles in developing working partnerships with the different organisations of the criminal justice agency.

Policing the two communities

In the last decade there has been a perception within certain sections of the Unionist/Loyalist community that the government has delivered a number of political, social and economic concessions to the Nationalist/Republican community. Therefore it was interesting to determine whether respondents had identified any differences in the methods of policing experienced by working class Republican and Loyalist communities. It was apparent that there was a perception that the PSNI viewed the two communities very differently and as such policed them in very diverse ways. According to respondents the police used more direct and forceful tactics in Loyalist areas compared with Republican communities:

I think there has been a perception that the police have turned to a softly softly approach in Republican working class areas. They nearly view Loyalist areas as 'you should know better and do what you are told' (Loyalist).

Graffiti has been etched on the walls in one Loyalist area that epitomises their views on the new dispensation for policing. The letters PSNI have been spelt out as Police Serving Nationalist Interests. There is a clear notion that police are only concerned with developing partnerships with Nationalists and Republicans and are unconcerned about issues in working class Loyalist communities.

One respondent went as far as to indicate that the police had become a sectarian organisation. Within their community the police were viewed as a growing Catholic organisation, only concerned with harassing young Protestants and arresting people from Loyalist areas:

They drive in here in their Land Rovers and open the back doors and call the women black bastards...they nearly run the kids over. They are anti-Protestant, its as if these new recruits have a bit of power and they want to take it out on this community (Loyalist).

It was evident from the discussions that there was a clear perception that the police treated Loyalist and Republican communities very differently. This was based on the attitudes and behaviours of officers policing in their communities. They were unaware of the tactics deployed in Republican areas but assumed that the radical changes to policing had benefited them more.

Existing community safety programmes

Several respondents were involved in community safety and restorative justice programmes in Loyalist communities. These include Neighbourhood Watch Schemes, local community safety partnerships, established at a neighbourhood level, and Shankill Alternatives. In recent years they have been involved in a number of initiatives that aimed to improve the quality of life for local residents, and to also develop and sustain relationships with the various agencies of the criminal justice system:

We are not here to police the community. That is the police's job. We are here to offer support, keep the community informed; provide a degree of accountability; influence policy makers and generally provide a link between the community and the police where appropriate (Community worker).

It was interesting to note that there continued to be those within Loyalist/Unionist communities who preferred not to use or engage with the police. In this respect the existing community safety groups have supported these individuals and facilitated engagement when required:

If we get information we have no problem taking it to the police…but we want to encourage people to go directly to the police, but if they need our support that is fine (Community worker).

One respondent associated with restorative justice discussed the complex issues facing their organisation in relation to working in partnership with the PSNI and other criminal justice organisations. Joint protocols have been established at a strategic level between the PSNI and the restorative programmes, and in theory this should allow for a joined up approach. However, in a more operational and practical environment the relationship between local neighbourhood officers and the programme workers is not replicating what has been agreed at the strategic level:

They are too rigid. The protocols are fine at the higher echelons of power but for the ordinary beat cop that information is not filtering down (Alternatives worker).

It was clear that the existing programmes of restorative justice and community safety have been addressing community issues and concerns around anti-social behaviour and criminality. Furthermore, they have been the catalyst for various levels of engagement between the local communities and the police. However, the PSNI response and commitment to these initiatives will ultimately determine their success. Issues around funding and resources will continue to influence their productivity. Strategically, the PSNI have acknowledged their importance, operationally it is crucial that they deliver on their commitments to work in partnership to address the community's concerns.

Loyalist paramilitaries

Attention then focused on the role of Loyalist paramilitaries within the context of community safety and criminality. In comparison to their Republican counterparts they have continued to have a prominent role within their communities, administering informal justice on occasions:

There was an absence of policing and when people needed help they went to the paramilitaries who were the ones who could deliver instant justice because there were no formal connections or relationships with the police (Loyalist).

It was noted that organisations such as Alternatives, based on a model of restorative justice, had made significant progress in addressing paramilitary punishments, and resolving disputes within Loyalist communities. However, according to several respondents there appeared to be a significant risk of local communities advocating the use of these punishments if their expectations were not delivered from the formal criminal justice system:

Local people have told me they have went to the paramilitaries...they have sorted their problems for them in a quick and uncomplicated manner (Community worker).

The key was for the police and other criminal justice agencies to attempt to meet the needs and expectations of the community. Interestingly, one respondent affiliated with a paramilitary organisation concluded that they no longer wanted the responsibility of policing the communities:

I'm trying to disempower paramilitarism but if the police are not responding then the communities are going to re-empower paramiliatrism...they are giving them their status back as community policemen...ironically, if you speak with paramilitaries they don't want to get involved, its not their fight anymore (Loyalist).

Loyalist paramilitaries are not as structured and coherent as their Republican counterparts. Each area has to some extent got their own degree of power and control, thus it was more complex devising a strategy of positive engagement that would be endorsed by all of the individuals associated with the different organisations. For years paramilitaries controlled local areas and benefited financially from a lack of policing, therefore it would be in the interests of some groups to continue the disengagement and apparent policing vacuum within these communities:

There will be elements that don't want to bring the police into the community because it is a threat to their position within the community (Unionist).

One method of promoting this disengagement was to continue to associate reporting crime as 'touting'. According to respondents there were still sections of the community who perceived informing the police about crime as 'touting'. Attempts were being made by community groups and representatives to remove this stigma, but it was acknowledged that this would take time. Interestingly, there appeared to be a tariff of offences that ultimately led to either reporting or not reporting crime:

If we know a rapist it is OK to tell the police, if we know a child abuser it is

OK to tell the police and you are not thought of as a tout. If you tell them about a drug dealer or paramilitary activity then you are a tout (Loyalist).

It is clear that Loyalist paramilitaries continue to exert a degree of control within certain communities. There is a general consensus that the majority of individuals associated with Loyalist paramilitaries no longer wish to be involved in administering punishments and policing their communities. They recognise that the PSNI can address issues of criminality with the support of the community. However, there continue to be those who do not want to relinquish the power they exert over their communities, and see the distancing of the police and local community as one method of maintaining their power base.

Facilitating engagement

The discussion focused on both responsibility and methods of developing relationships between the PSNI and local communities. There appeared to be three central elements in the development of relationships, the PSNI themselves, the community, and finally outside organisations. A number of respondents felt that one area where the PSNI could do more centred on the appearance and accessibility of police stations. There was recognition that there was a continued threat from dissident Republicans on the PSNI, however, there was a general consensus that the current image of the police was still security focused and to a degree militaristic:

I would see the police as hiding behind their armour plated walls. The police haven't realised that the war is over. They need to take down their walls and put out their signs 'POLICE' and create the environment where the public can simply walk in (Unionist).

In working class communities where the police appear to have fractured relationships, the police stations are more like fortresses with the aim of keeping people out rather than encouraging them to enter. They remain intimidating environments, places that restrict the integration between the community and the police. However, one respondent felt that the current appearance of police stations reflected the realties of society, and until we addressed the legacy of the past it would be foolish to remove all of the security mechanisms:

We have not addressed all of the underlying problems that separate us in Northern Ireland…we have managed our problems but we have not resolved them (Unionist).

There was also an indication that the PSNI could do more to facilitate relationships, such as attending community events and participating in local social activities. There was a realisation that much of this was dependent upon capacity and resources, but according to respondents there was a willingness from communities for the police to actively participate in their activities:

They have a wonderful opportunity to build relationships with people. The community really want to engage with the police. They could attend social events in the centres…get to know the community, and let the community get to know the police…they have to get out of their stations and meet people (Unionist).

All of the responsibility for engagement was not placed solely on the PSNI. There was a rationale for communities themselves to actively encourage the establishment of positive working partnerships with the police:

There is a problem with policing in Loyalist areas…and those people do have very legitimate complaints but they also have to take some of the responsibility to improve that (Community worker).

Communities have the knowledge base to provide the police with the information to develop strategic and practical plans to address their issues and concerns. For years sections of the community have failed to engage or participate in discussions on policing and community safety. It was something that was taken for granted, not really an issue. However, there is a growing realisation that communities can no longer expect the police to police.

In relation to the role of independent organisations facilitating relationships between the community and the police much of the attention focused on the impact of District Policing Partnerships. One of the first criticisms of the DPPs centred on their makeup and essentially how much they represented the views and interests of working class Loyalist communities:

There are people on them who don't live around here. How are they supposed to fight for our rights, they cannot relate to me or my family…it is a middle class forum debating middle class issues (Loyalist).

Furthermore, there appeared to be a distinct lack of knowledge about the roles and responsibilities of a DPP. There was an awareness that they could monitor the local police, but very little else was known in relation to the work they do. The majority of interviewees had not attended public meetings because they were unaware of where or when they took place:

I don't actually know what they do…they are another toothless quango. What do they achieve? They come up with a yearly action plan that isn't even relevant (Community worker).

The key to developing the relationships between the police and local communities has centred on the local communities and the police along with outside organisations such as DPPs. Combined they can provide the support and energy to develop the working partnerships that are crucial in allowing the PSNI to address issues of criminality and community safety.

Police priorities

Developing policing priorities was a relatively new concept to the majority of respondents and indeed the wider Unionist/Loyalist community. Throughout the conflict the security forces were highly visible and whether it was the reality or not there was a notion that the police would respond to every inquiry. However, in this post-conflict society and under the new dispensation for policing the PSNI's agenda is somewhat driven by budget and resource issues, therefore the realities of policing were not compatible with what the community expected. A central criticism focused on the prioritisation of calls and the use of resources. What was viewed as important to communities did not appear to be a priority to the PSNI. This was often reflected in the resources they committed to specific operations, or the fact that neighbourhood or community officers were usually the first to be sacrificed for other operations:

There is a notion that they treat anti-social behaviour as something that can be handled by their neighbourhood teams. If a pensioner calls them, they don't come out, yet the incident is ruining the life of the pensioner…by the time someone calls the problems has gone it needed to be acted upon at the time (Community worker).

The PSNI constantly talk about policing with the community and the development of positive partnerships. However, respondents did not feel that the idea of community policing was a significant priority in the overall strategic planning of the PSNI. Respondents indicated that there was a distinct lack of knowledge in the community about what the PSNI meant by community policing. In most cases when groups had developed a relationship with a specific officer that officer was soon shifted to another division or role within the organisation. Furthermore, when there was a specific 'crisis in the area' like knife crime or car crime, the community/neighbourhood officers appeared to be expendable in their existing capacity and allocated new priorities:

You know, you start to develop a relationship and they attend your functions, then there is some big story in the papers around drugs or something and the officers can't meet because their boss has them on other duties (Unionist).

It appeared that the community's priorities did not often match those of the police. A key tenet of policing is the development of relationships at the neighbourhood level. However, according to respondents the idea of community policing is being paid lip service by a number of officers and is not viewed as a significant priority within the context of the new dispensation for policing.

Political leadership

It was important to gain an understanding of the types of political support for these communities, and assess the different types of initiatives and programmes that have been advocated to develop relationships with the police. It immediately became apparent that whereas Republican communities had Sinn Féin to champion their rights and strategically influence policies, Loyalist working class areas did not appear to have a similar form of leadership. There appeared to be more fragmentation with support for different Unionist and Independent political parties which ultimately meant that there was not one coherent voice campaigning for these communities, an example being the Progressive Unionist Party who garner much of their support from Loyalist working class communities and champion the rights of these communities yet have only one elected representative in Stormont. According to respondents elected representatives appeared to shy away from issues pertaining to policing and Loyalist communities:

The Unionist politicians will not stand up and defend the Loyalist working class communities if the police go in heavy handed…these people feel alone and open to abuse (Loyalist).

The arguments surrounding the poor political support for Loyalist working class communities also focused on the impact of the DPPs.

Previously it was alluded that there was a degree of apathy from the community towards these partnerships. One respondent familiar with the workings of the partnerships drew comparisons between public meetings in Loyalist and Republican communities. They concluded that those representing Republican areas were more vocal, committed and passionate about policing issues compared to those apparently representing the voice of Loyalist areas:

I think that the DPPs have become very Council orientated, very much controlled by the local councillors. However, I can imagine that the DPP meetings in West Belfast are far more vibrant than the ones in North Down (Unionist).

The lack of leadership within Loyalist working class communities is not a new phenomenon. This is not to say that there are not prominent individuals working diligently within these communities developing partnerships with the police at both a strategic and operational level. However, these communities are missing a voice at the strategic forums which have the mechanisms to both hold to account and challenge the police.

Public Prosecution Service

There were several concerns about the role of the PPS, but more importantly the lack of information that emanated from the organisation. This focused on two areas, information related to the decision making process in a general sense, and secondly the level of communication and information for victims of crime:

The PPS is a bit of a mystery. None of us are quiet sure how it works, or how it makes its decisions (Community worker).

Within communities there was confusion as to what was required for prosecutions to take place against known offenders. There was awareness that the police were only responsible for so much, but communities did not understand how the PPS decided to prosecute specific cases:

One fella is constantly stealing cars and being arrested, yet he isn't prosecuted…other wee lad gets lifted for fighting; next you know he is up in court (Loyalist).

The lack of consistency in prosecutions was not only confusing it was creating an environment where local people questioned the motives of both the PPS and the alleged offenders. There was a perception that repeat offenders who were not prosecuted had been recruited as informers by the PSNI and were 'touting' on the community. This was potentially dangerous for the individual concerned as there was no evidence to back up these perceptions.

In relation to individual incidents respondents recounted instances where victims had not been informed that the alleged offender in their case had been released or not charged with the offence. This was highly sensitive and emotional for the individual/family involved and highlighted the damage the PPS can do to the credibility of the criminal justice system.

According to respondents the majority of people are aware that the PPS are entirely independent of the PSNI. However, their actions have the potential to undermine the positive work of the police in developing and sustaining relationships and working partnerships within local communities.

Summary

There is a minimal amount of research that documents the perceptions of the Unionist/Loyalist communities towards the police and also their levels of engagement and participation in policing-led programmes and initiatives. From the discussions it became apparent that the legacy of the conflict had a significant impact on how these communities viewed the police. There was a fragmentation within Loyalist communities during the conflict with those supporting paramilitaries disengaging with the formal criminal justice system. Those that did not support Loyalist paramilitaries were nevertheless encouraged not to engage with the police or develop any meaningful forms of relationships.

One consequence of the Troubles was the movement of police officers away from the Loyalist working class communities. The knock-on effect was that these communities began to lose their affiliation and identity with the police, along with an argument that the police could not identify with the issues and concerns that were prevalent within working class communities as they did not reside within them. This, compounded with the policing of parades and the political changes, has led to a complete disengagement in some communities with the police.

Positive experiences of policing are at a minimum, and there is some suspicion from some sections of Loyalism that the interests of their communities are being left behind in pursuit of the support and endorsement of the Republican communities for policing. There have been attempts to develop relationships and build positive partnerships, but these have come from the community and are largely built upon personalities and specific individuals. There does not appear to be a coherent strategy of engagement from the police in relation to building associations and links with Loyalist working class communities.

The lack of support at a political level for facilitating relationships between these communities and the police was also noticeable, especially when compared with the impact of Sinn Féin within Republican working class communities. It is obvious that the existing mechanisms for building and sustaining links between the community and the police are not working, and the notion of 'community policing' has not resonated within Loyalist working class areas.

6. Police Officers' Views

A number of discussions were conducted with police officers from both an operational and strategic background. The majority of officers from Neighbourhood and Response Teams were situated in the Greater Belfast area. Further discussions at a Command level took place with officers strategically involved in policing all districts in Northern Ireland.

The following section documents the key findings from discussions with police officers there. A number of themes that emerged from these discussions and have been outlined below.

Legacy of the past

Discussions with several interviewees revealed a number of issues in relation to the past, and the legacy of the conflict. Discussions focused on two key areas, firstly the experiences of officers policing in communities that historically, as a result of the conflict, had not engaged with the police, and, secondly, the impact on the resources of the PSNI of the need to review historical police investigations into incidents before the paramilitary ceasefires.

There was a sense of acknowledgement from several officers that incidents in the past had shaped people's thoughts and perceptions of contemporary policing, and that it was important to recognise the events that had shaped society:

The legacy of the past is a big concern for communities. It is not something you can just simply put under the rug and move on and say 'look we've a new dispensation now, we are a new police' (PSNI representative-Command)

All of the police officers recognised the emotive issues raised both within communities and the police themselves in relation to the Troubles. There was a realisation that historical events had the potential to undermine the future of policing in Northern Ireland if they were not addressed. It was interesting to note that officers who had experience of policing through the Troubles noted a distinct lack of trust and confidence from communities in the policing structures, and that these were themes that required immediate attention and constant resources. Respondents felt that communities' perceptions of the police, especially within many Nationalist and Republican communities, were formed largely on their experiences throughout the Troubles, and for many this was negative.

Large sections of the community continued to associate past policing with collusion and the recruitment of informers.

A number of officers discussed in depth the impact that the growing call for public inquiries and historical investigations was having on the resources and the capacity of the PSNI. Reference was made to the Cory Collusion Inquiry and his recommendation for public inquiries into the murders of six individuals including Pat Finucane, Robert Hamill, Rosemary Nelson and Billy Wright (HMSO, 2004). There was a feeling from some that the constant re-examination of the past was restricting the organisation's ability to move forward and deliver a representative and accountable policing service in a post-conflict society:

We are supposed to be looking forward...not continually looking over our shoulder, dealing with the historical stuff. At some stage there has to be no more inquiries, lets try and get this thing working as it was envisaged eight years ago (PSNI representative - Operational).

A recent media story reflected the views from the head of the PSNI whereby Northern Ireland's most senior police officer acknowledged the detrimental impact the analysis of the past was having on their organisation: *'Orde: Public inquiries hindering PSNI's policing duties'* (Belfast Telegraph, 05.07.07). In the article the Chief Constable noted that it was costing the equivalent of 250 officers to sift through records and monitor sensitive information. He felt that this was one of the main threats to providing good policing and meeting criminal targets.

It was apparent from the discussions that there had to be a balance found between developing both an understanding and acknowledgement of the past, and continuing to outline and present a model of policing that embraced the future. This notion of drawing a line in the sand in relation to investigating the past was supported by a large number of interviewees but they also recognised the importance in addressing people's concerns. The Oversight Commissioner for Northern Ireland in his final report (2007) included a section entitled 'A Choice: Policing the Past, or Policing the Future?' There is a realisation that this is an extremely emotive issue, but the question has been asked as to what is the most appropriate mechanism for addressing the concerns of everyone with a vested interest in policing.

Existing community safety programmes

A key element of the discussions focused on the role of existing community safety programmes within the context of the formal criminal justice system. Throughout the Troubles both Loyalist and Republican communities established different community-based initiatives in response to issues and concerns around community safety. These developments included Restorative Justice Schemes, Interface Forums, Mobile Phone Networks, and Safer Neighbourhood Partnerships. Officers were asked whether these programmes were complementary with the aims and objectives of the criminal justice system, and whether they could work in partnership with the PSNI.

According to a number of police officers, within several Republican areas members of the public were using the community-based organisations as conduits between themselves and the police:

You find that everyone to some extent is working together…in some of these schemes, people will report crime to them then they will forward it on to the police (Police representative - Operational).

There was an acknowledgement that some people continued to be reluctant to engage formally with the police, but through the guidance and support of the community programmes were willing to engage when necessary. Furthermore, respondents recognised the benefits of these existing programmes to the police's mission of delivering community policing. These existing networks provided the foundation for the police to build relationships within the communities:

Policing is now a partnership, you know police cannot do it on their own, they never could…so it has to be the community, the police, all the voluntary and statutory agents coming together to make it work (PSNI representative - Strategic).

There was some hesitancy from several respondents on the future relationships between community-based programmes and the criminal justice system. There was a realisation that we were still in a relative 'honeymoon' period, and that developing relationships was a priority. However, in the past a number of the community-based organisations operated with a degree of autonomy. In essence they were established in response to disengagement with the police, but were now expected to operate in a climate where the police were the recognised deliverers of law and order. There was a degree of concern from some respondents as to how this new partnership approach was going to pan out.

Discussions soon focused on the relationship between the police and community restorative justice programmes (CRJ). As previously noted the police had an existing working relationship with Alternatives, the restorative justice programme based within Loyalist communities. However, Community Restorative Justice Ireland (CRJI), the Republican based approach, historically had no ties with police or the criminal justice system. According to a number of interviewees in recent months there had been strong partnerships developing between CRJI and the police in regards to the sharing of information. This relationship has strengthened since the Chief Inspector of Criminal Justice conducted inspections of the community-based restorative justice schemes in Loyalist (CJINI, 2007) and Republican (CJINI, 2008) areas, with the schemes being accredited by the Northern Ireland Office. They have established formalised protocols for working with statutory agencies especially the PSNI. Recent media reports have highlighted this close co-operation: *'200 Crimes reported via CRJ to the police'* (Irish News, 04.01.08). A significant number of these cases were sexual assaults, burglaries and drug related crimes.

There was general agreement from all of the interviewees that there was organisational support for all of the restorative programmes as long as they adhered to the rule of law:

If they are run correctly, and there is no threat of paramilitary trappings and associations with them...as long as they're not associated with paramilitaries (PSNI representative - Operational).

However, there were other respondents who felt that CRJI in a number of incidents were selecting what information to pass onto the police, restricting access to specific individuals and only half entering into a process of engagement:

I think the cases that they are giving us, they are testing the waters. I think they are being careful in what they are giving us. They are watching how it is being handled (PSNI representative - Operational).

There was an acceptance from respondents that these community based initiatives had an important role within the context of policing and community safety, as long as they adhered to the rule of law. According to the police officers a significant amount of their time was being spent responding to incidents of anti-social behaviour and more specifically youths causing annoyance:

Most of the time we are responding to calls from residents about kids running around the estates, drinking or just out in large groups (PSNI representative – Operational)

The police recognised the effect these incidents were having on local communities, but also acknowledged the impact on their resources and time. There was a realisation that existing community programmes had developed the contacts and had mechanisms in place to address their communities' concerns and that these could complement the roles and responsibilities of the police.

Threats and intimidation

Discussions soon focused on the threats to police. A number of events in recent years including the shooting of a police officer in Derry/Londonderry as he dropped his child off at school by a Loyalist group (BBC News, 23.07.07), and the car bombing of a PSNI constable near Castlederg by dissident Republicans (Belfast Telegraph, 13.05.08) have resulted in the police reassessing their security threat. Furthermore, statistics released from the PSNI revealed that from June 2007 – June 2008 sixteen serving police officers were advised to leave their homes because of a direct terrorist threat (Belfast Telegraph, 25.08.08).

One visible manifestation of this has been the reintroduction of flak jackets in some parts of Northern Ireland, mainly in the Greater Belfast area (The Guardian, 13.12.07). According to all of the respondents there was a credible threat against serving police officers. There was recognition that on occasions this may inhibit or restrict their ability to deliver on their roles and responsibilities, but there had to be a balance between the safety of the officer and the needs of the public:

It is a very difficult judgement call between the health and safety of our employees and then how we effectively deliver a service to the public (PSNI representative - Strategic).

We will take some defensive measures but they will not be intrusive, they will not prevent us from going out and doing out main job (PSNI representative - Strategic).

Recent increased threats had resulted in significant changes to the appearance and routines of police officers. There had been increased patrols in both Belfast and Derry/Londonderry with a number of vehicle checkpoints uncharacteristically springing up in these cities. These actions were unfamiliar to a number of people who had become accustomed to the more relaxed mode of policing employed in the last ten years:

We have got officers back in flak jackets, they are back double patrolling, they're back in armoured vehicles, it's a huge step back for policing…we have had to draw back from community engagement slightly (PSNI representative - Strategic).

One officer reflected on the recent changes in both their uniform and daily duties since the heightened security threat. It was refreshing to note that some officers had been serving in the police and had never experienced a threat against them:

We are all wary of the dissident threat. For a while there we all wore yellow coats, now we are back wearing ballistic body armour again and stuff which is alien to a lot of new officers (PSNI representative – Operational).

Respondents were asked to comment on whether they felt that the security threat could impact on their ability to deliver a 'normal' police service:

It does create difficulties…but I keep telling people don't look at this as in terms of what happened last year or two years ago. Instead look at the progress in the last decade or twenty years (PSNI representative – Strategic).

A number of respondents felt it was important to indicate that the threats would not be a significant factor in restricting their ability to deliver community policing. There was a view that there was limited support from within communities for the dissident paramilitary groups, and that too much progress had been made to date in relation to encouraging communities to both embrace and participate in local policing.

Engaging with Republican communities

Discussions around relationships between Republican communities focused on two key topics, the impact of Sinn Féin signing up to policing, and the level of engagement between the police and Republican communities at the grass roots, non-political level. The engagement of Sinn Féin within the context of policing and criminal justice has meant that the police have found it easier to police in Republican areas:

We now have dialogue with groups who never spoke with us…we are patrolling in areas that we were not welcome in, in all there is more demand for policing (PSNI representative - Strategic).

Beforehand there was very little in the way of meetings or face to face contacts with residents groups, community groups, women's associations…but now we are meeting on a weekly basis with all these groups (PSNI representative - Operational).

Within the context of the community as a whole engaging with the police and being comfortable contacting them and reporting crime it was recognised that this would take time:

They have lived through thirty years of 'don't report to the police', 'don't bring the police into the area'…now we are probably in transition, it will take time (PSNI representative - Operational).

There have been a number of high profile steps from both Republicans and the police to encourage the wider community to engage with all agencies of the criminal justice system. The symbolic nature of the historic meeting when the Chief Constable was invited to attend a meeting in West Belfast with representatives from Republican and Nationalist communities on issues around anti-social behaviour (BBC News, 04.07.07) is one example of strategic engagement between Sinn Féin, the Republican community and the police:

It is all about reassurance and confidence…so people can come forward and report things. There are small steps being taken and things are slowly getting there, and people's confidence will increase (PSNI representative - Strategic).

Several respondents talked about how policing in some Republican areas was very different than others, that not all Republican communities immediately began to engage in meaningful dialogue and interaction with the police. It appeared that engagement was more positive, and communities more willing to participate with the policing structures when there was a clear and visible need. This was highlighted by the recent feud in the Ballymurphy housing estate in West Belfast in 2006/07 (BBC News, 04.10.06). If there were incidents of violent crime, anti-social behaviour or drug related problems then communities became more responsive. However, in Republican areas where there did not appear to be the same need, engagement was more minimal and relations slightly more chilled. This was illustrated by the lack positive relationships in Castlederg (Hamilton, et al 2008).

A number of interviewees, although impressed with the level of commitment shown from Republicans to policing, continued to reserve their final judgement on the relationship between policing and the

Republican community. They noted the great deal of progress made, but acknowledged that the process was only eighteen months old, and would require a long term approach for stability to be assured. They were adopting a cautious approach and were interested in how they would engage with the police over contentious issues such as parades and interface violence:

To date Republicans have been very positive and responsive but I still think there is the potential for the relationships to be tested (PSNI representative - Operational).

Police officers were asked whether they felt the Republican community were fully engaged and committed to policing. There were mixed views, generally it was accepted that Sinn Féin had shown leadership and direction. However, several respondents felt that at a grass roots level local communities continued to show a reluctance to engage with the police. They attributed this to a number of factors including a lack of knowledge about the roles and responsibility of the police; continued stereotyping of past policing; and a degree of empathy with policing and the wider criminal justice structures:

I still don't believe the community feel free. I think it is still coming from the fear aspect as opposed to being reluctant. I don't think that they are getting that clear message (PSNI representative - Operational).

Officers were also asked whether they had difficulties in developing relationships with Republicans and in some instances ex-combatants. Generally, interviewees noted that it was difficult on occasions, because during the course of the Troubles 302 police officers were killed and many more seriously injured as a result of paramilitary violence. However, there was a realisation that both sides had to engage at both a strategic and operational level for the benefit of everyone. This relationship would take time to develop and stabilise, and both sides had to earn the respect and trust of each other.

Engaging with Loyalist communities

The focus soon moved on to issues surrounding the level of engagement between the police and members of the Loyalist community. The first observation highlighted by respondents was the perceived lack of political leadership within the Loyalist communities. The distinction was made with the Republican community, and the impact of Sinn Féin at a strategic and operational level on policing. There did not appear to be the same representation for Loyalist working class communities:

There's not the same sort of political representation as in Republican communities. They do not have the support, or people fighting their corner (PSNI representative – Operational).

Politically there is more of a split within Loyalist communities, therefore they don't have the same clout (PSNI representative - Operational).

One key event that a number of respondents discussed in detail was the impact of the Whiterock riots in Belfast in September 2005 and the subsequent disengagement of many Protestant community groups and Loyalist representatives in discussions and participation with the police:

A number of communities just stopped engagement, there was nothing…the communities were not encouraged to communicate with the police by elements within those Loyalist areas (PSNI representative - Strategic).

There was a perception within those communities that the police had over-reacted and used excessive force during a parade and the subsequent disturbances. In a number of areas the police were unable to attend community events or in some cases deliver programmes within Protestant schools. However, in recent months relationships had improved, and the police were again developing positive working partnerships with the majority of community groups:

I would say that people might not have a good perception of the police, but instead would have a normal perception (PSNI representative - Operational).

There was also an acknowledgement that similar to the Republican community there were certain elements in the Loyalist community that refused to support the police and criminal justice system and would continue to pursue a policy of disengagement to promote their own self interests:

There are people with no respect for law and order, they have their own agenda to push and don't want to see the community engaging with the police (PSNI representative - Strategic).

There was also a view that potentially sections of the Loyalist community may feel that there is a stronger emphasis within the PSNI on building relations with the Republican community as opposed to the Loyalist one:

I feel Loyalism is feeling a little left out. They are feeling a bit wounded and they are starting to say that we (PSNI) are putting too much effort into the one side (Republicans) (PSNI representative - Operational).

Although there is no evidence to support this theory, discussions with representatives from Loyalist communities revealed that there was a perception that the police were encouraging engagement and extending resources more so towards Republican areas:

It may well be that one community, the Nationalist community, maybe starts to see a constructive engagement and increasing confidence with the police while the other community for different reasons feels maybe that their voice isn't being heard (PSNI representative).

There is a degree of suspicion within sections of the Loyalist community that the police are encouraged to 'reach out' to the Republican community and concentrate resources on addressing community safety issues. There are some within the Loyalist community who view policing in a similar manner to other political changes that have occurred in Northern Ireland in the last decade. They maintain that they are being left behind and that Nationalists and Republicans are constantly being rewarded. The police continue to deal with the legacy of the reform of the organisation including the name change and the impact of the Whiterock riots in 2005. For years sections within the Loyalist community had an affinity with the police, they could clearly identify with the organisation and there was an assumption that it was solely there for their protection within the context of the conflict. However, since the political and social changes experienced by Northern Ireland in the post-conflict era the Loyalist people have lost the emotional, social and community-based ties they once had with the police.

Police resources

A topical theme centred on the levels of resources available to the police. There was general agreement from all of the officers that there was a distinct lack of police resources. The discussion was placed within the context of the increased demand for policing:

One of the real challenges police officers have is managing the demand with the decreasing resources available to us…that is the big pressure, meeting the needs of the community (PSNI representative - Strategic).

Since Sinn Féin endorsed policing there has been an entirely new section of the community that have begun to use and access police resources. This, combined with the significant decrease in the number of police officers since the Patten reforms, has resulted in more people wanting to use the police but there being fewer officers to respond:

It is not a state secret that this organisation is smaller than it used to be, it is not a state secret that we used to rely heavily on the army. In the past less people phoned the police...but now there are less officers and more calls, we are prioritising calls just like our colleagues in England and Wales (PSNI representative).

In the past prioritisation was not part of the policing dictionary in Northern Ireland. The security budget was practically unlimited and the police, with the support of the army, were in a position to respond to every emergency call out. However, in the new era of policing, like so many public service agencies, resources and funding had become significant factors. It should be noted that the police strength currently stands at approximately 7,500 officers, but a recent report from Her Majesty's Inspectorate of Constabulary indicated that by 2011 the numbers of police officers should be reduced from 7,500 to approximately 6,000 (Belfast Telegraph, 17.01.07). The implications for the decrease in police numbers are that there will be an even greater tension between the demand for policing and resources against the expectations of the community.

Community Policing

Following on from the conversations around police resources attention turned to the development and implication of community policing which was so central to the ethos of police reform put forward by Patten. It soon became apparent that there were mixed views around the levels of importance the police placed on neighbourhood and community policing:

I'm on the bottom rung and neighbourhood policing isn't a priority as such until it has to be, and then it's go out and be seen (PSNI representative - Operational).

We have always had strong community engagement, it is crucial to develop confidence in the organisation. You do this by being seen and interacting with the public (PSNI representative - Operational).

According to officers, due to a lack of resources, specifically police officers, community policing was often sidelined or given less of a priority at a command level. This was in stark contrast to what police officers were experiencing on the ground, where communities were keen to engage with the police on community-based issues:

What we are seeing now is a greater willingness from community representatives to make us more aware of issues in their area, in particular issues like drugs, under-age drinking...there's a greater willingness now for communities to start to challenge police and ask, what can you do for us? (PSNI representative - Operational)

One officer felt that community policing was not being given enough credence within the organisation, and that at a leadership level there was not enough direction or emphasis placed on it. It was recognised that it was an important facet of policing, but there did not appear to be a long term strategic vision being employed by the organisation as a whole. They were critical of the 'tick box' policing driven by performance indicators, spread sheets and percentages:

I think the organisation is confused. Community police officers are becoming pigeon-holed and there is competition between immediate results and the more long term approach to developing relationships. The bosses want results now, without the wait (PSNI representative - Operational)

It was also interesting to note that one officer felt that as the security threat diminished the environment and political climate would be more suitable for community policing initiatives:

As the security situation improves rather than police officers retreating all the way back into the stations, we would be encouraging them to take their breaks in local cafes, and be seen within the community (PSNI representative - Operational).

It was clear from the discussions that community policing was an area that had the potential to cause the most debate within the organisation. There appeared to be a degree of confusion surrounding the importance of community policing within the organisation and how much strategic and operational importance it actually had.

Community expectations

Discussions soon turned to issues around the police's ability to deliver on their roles and responsibilities within the context of an expectant community. In recent years with the absence of organised paramilitary control in Republican and Loyalist communities, and the new political dispensation there has been a heightened expectation in communities that policing, given the current climate, would be in a position to finally deliver within a normal environment. According to respondents there has been a significant increase in police call outs:

There is more demand in certain areas…its fair to say that not only is there more demand, but also heightened expectations (PSNI representative - Strategic).

One recent news article highlighted the extent of the demand for policing in Northern Ireland. The story noted that one call was made every three minutes or 173,000 calls to the PSNI non-emergency number in a twelve-month period (Belfast Telegraph, 29.11.07)

There was an acknowledgement that although it was positive that people were contacting the police, ultimately this placed increased pressure on their ability to respond to all of the inquiries. This was the concern of several officers, in that people might be calling the police for the very first time, but the police are unable to respond because of a resource or capacity issue. This in turn would damage the reputation of the organisation and provide people with the opportunity to question why they should engage with the police:

People from a Republican background could be calling us for the first time ever…say something big is happening at the same time and we cannot get out…what's that individual going think of us…they probably will not call again (PSNI representative - Operational).

A number of respondents talked about the impact television programmes were having in increasing community expectations of policing and what it could deliver. This was especially true in areas where historically local communities had little or no experience of formal methods of policing or the criminal justice system:

The critical point for me is now people have an image of what they think policing is, some of it comes from the television…a lot of it is not realistic. On TV they condense it into one hour, in reality policing can be boring and take ages. People get frustrated because their expectations are not being met (PSNI representative - Strategic).

Managing people's expectations was viewed by all respondents as one of the key goals for the organisation. Normal policing in Western societies is about prioritising resources and responding to emergencies. There is a danger that people will expect the police to be able to respond to all issues pertaining to crime and community safety, especially in those communities that have not experienced policing. Officers were asked whether they felt that communities would attempt to resurrect the mechanisms of informal justice delivered in the past by paramilitaries. Their view from their experience on the ground was that there did not appear to be the willingness from communities to resort to this form of punishment, but it was acknowledged that there was the potential if the police and other criminal justice agencies did not deliver and manage the community's expectations.

It was also interesting to note that community negativity towards the police may not simply be a reaction to their expectations not being met. As we move from a peace process into a post-conflict society it is possible that some of the issues that separated communities disappear and more normal issues surface. There was a view that class was a significant factor in attitudes and experiences of policing. A community's expectations were becoming negative regardless of their community background, and they simply refused to engage with the police because of their perceived social standing:

Often people don't want to report crime to the police. That's not a Protestant or Catholic thing…it is more a working class issue, one that you experience throughout the world (PSNI representative - Strategic).

The expectations surrounding policing in Northern Ireland are extremely high. For one section of the community, there is the novelty of engaging with and accessing an organisation that they had no prior experience of. For the remaining community there is the process of re-engagement with an organisation that they no longer identify or relate with. Both communities have high expectations of the police. They have been informed at the highest political level that this is the most accountable, transparent and professional police service in the word. They expect a service that will deliver on crime and community safety. However, the police realise that these expectations must be managed and viewed within a measure of reality, and communities must understand that terms such as prioritisation, capacity, and resources will determine how these expectations are met.

Partnerships

There was general agreement from the officers that for the police to deliver a positive and successful service they required the support, participation and commitment of voluntary, community and statutory organisations. There was an acknowledgement that the police could not be responsible for all aspects of community safety:

There is a realisation and an acknowledgement that the police cannot do it on their own, we need help (PSNI representation - Strategic).

More importantly the police did not want ownership over programmes and initiatives aimed at improving community safety and alleviating the fear of crime. They wanted to work in conjunction with the community, support different programmes and offer resources, guidance and expertise where appropriate. It was interesting to note that several interviewees felt that the police needed to improve their methods of developing partnerships and relationships within the community:

We need to get better…we have got to engage with other people, not just the public but other public sector bodies, voluntary groups and actually start some real partnership work (PSNI representative - Operational).

Several respondents used the example of the SOS Bus **(www.sosbusni.com)** which is a collaboration of the main emergency services in Northern Ireland along with local businesses and community and statutory groups. The project is based on models that have been developed in England and is a response to increased levels of alcohol and substance abuse by young people and rising levels of anti-social behaviour in city centres. This was a concrete example of the police developing sustainable relationships with other groups, and highlighted the significant progress society had made in recent years.

There was an acknowledgement from a number of officers that a key element to the success of partnerships was the establishment of relationships with the same people over a long period of time. In those areas where officers experienced a positive working relationship with community groups and other statutory agencies it was apparent that there was familiarisation with individuals. However, officers felt this was not consistent throughout Northern Ireland and indicated that a continual movement of personnel within the organisation restricted the development of partnerships:

There must be a frustration there from a partner perspective that they just don't have the consistency of relationship with a specific police officer (PSNI representative - Operational).

One officer commented that the significant changes that the police had undergone, along with the high numbers of new recruits, was a key element in the lack of consistent successful partnerships:

We are an incredibly young organisation at the minute in terms of service, and that automatically means you're going to find people being promoted, moving on to a different job etc (PSNI representative - Strategic).

There was a clear message from the police officers that the development of positive working partnerships was crucial for the delivery of a successful police service. As previously noted, the police were more than willing to embrace existing community safety initiatives and provide further expertise, resources and services where appropriate. However, there had to be a balance between these initiatives and the roles and responsibilities of the police who were the only organisation upholding the rule of law.

District Policing Partnerships

A number of issues were raised in relation to the impact of District Policing Partnerships on policing and whether they had positively contributed to policing and improved community safety in local areas. According to the police officers DPPs were viewed as having two key responsibilities, developing accountability and facilitating relationships. There was a sense of agreement from the majority of respondents that the concept underpinning DPPs was both positive and beneficial to both the police and local communities:

I think the concept is something that you cannot fault. The reality is that there needs to be some sort of bridge between the community and policing (PSNI representative - Operational).

With regards to the level of public interest in DPPs, there was an acknowledgement that the public meetings had generally been poorly attended:

I have attended meetings where there's no members of the public there at all…you are obviously not getting the message out (PSNI representative - Operational).

Two explanations were offered for this lack of engagement, one centred on the view that large sections of the public were uninterested in policing and criminal justice so therefore had no need to attend the meetings.

Secondly, there was a perception that the format of the public meetings was not appealing to the general public to either attend or contribute. One interviewee felt that the meetings were very formal, over complicated and did not encourage audience participation:

I don't think that the community feel that the meetings answer their questions…the feedback I am getting is that it is too complicated and formal, that's why people aren't attending (PSNI representative - Operational).

There was a willingness from the police to engage with local communities through the forums of the public meetings:

We would absolutely love it if the local community were there…It is just unfortunate that we are not getting that buy-in (PSNI representative - Strategic).

In relation to the role and function of the DPPs there was support for the accountability role that DPPs were bringing to local policing. It was recognised that historically policing had been viewed by large sections of the community as being secretive, partial and biased but it was hoped that through DPPs the public would have an opportunity to monitor and question the decisions undertaken by the police. It was interesting to note that there was a degree of criticism around the secondary role of the DPPs which concerned their level of engagement in developing community relationships:

In the time that I have been with the DPPs I haven't seen an awful lot that the DPP have done in terms of pro-active engagement (PSNI representative - Strategic)

According to a number of interviewees there was a degree of expectation within the PSNI that DPPs would be a key mechanism in facilitating relationships between the police and community at a local level. However, it became apparent from the discussions that there was limited practical evidence of DPPs providing the catalyst for this engagement. As one respondent noted:

I think the balance is moving too much towards accountability and DPPs are focusing less and less on engagement (PSNI representative - Operational).

A further interviewee felt that in recent months DPPs had lost their way in relation to what they were originally established to deliver:

I think that DPPs are seen by some people as a one way system of big brother on the police, it's not what they were set up to be; it's not what they should aim to be, what they should aim to be is the point of interaction with the police (PSNI representative - Strategic).

Discussions also focused on the impact Sinn Féin taking their place on DPPs would have in relation to policing. All of the interviewees welcomed the developments around policing within the Republican community. There was a strong view that now that Sinn Féin were represented on the Policing Board and DPPs then there would be opportunities to develop relationships and engagement with new communities, previously hostile to policing. It was also stated that there were independent members on the DPP from Republican communities and this was viewed positively as a further opportunity to reach out and debate issues on policing and community safety. Recent media attention has focused on Republican activists participating in the new policing and criminal justice structures: *'Former IRA POW to go on the DPP'* (North Belfast News, 05.04.08). It was reported that a former Republican prisoner who had been imprisoned in the Maze during the Troubles and who recently had been involved in community work had become an Independent member of the North Belfast DPP.

There was a degree of awareness from the respondents that there had to be a mechanism to facilitate relationships between the police and communities at a local level. The DPPs were viewed as integral in this process and a welcome contribution to the delivery of policing and raising awareness around issues of community safety. However, on reflection there was a sense of frustration from a number of interviewees that an opportunity was being wasted, in that DPPs were not being pro-active enough in developing relationships within local communities. Previous Sinn Féin and Republican disengagement from the process was viewed as restricting the overall effectiveness of DPPs. However since Sinn Féin and independent members from a Republican background were now fully participating in the process it was anticipated that this could prove the catalyst to delivering the objectives of DPPs that had been envisaged within the Patten report.

Public Prosecution Service / Judiciary

Discussions surrounding the role of the PPS and the judiciary in relation to policing proved very illuminating. It became apparent from an early stage that respondents felt that the PPS could do more to highlight their role in the criminal justice system and inform the public of the methods they applied to determine whether an individual was prosecuted or not. There was a degree of criticism from respondents who felt that the police were often viewed by the public as the representatives of the criminal justice system and therefore responsible if an individual was not prosecuted or received a not guilty verdict:

We still carry the can because the only part of the criminal justice system that really engages through the media with the public is the police (PSNI representative –Strategic).

According to the police officers, there is a constant attempt to highlight the different roles and responsibilities of the various agencies involved in the criminal justice system:

We are trying constantly at community meetings to tell them that all our job is to collect the evidence…we do not make recommendations anymore…We have a guy who sits in court every day and will fight for bail conditions or to keep them inside…he is coming out to a community meeting with me today to explain the difficulties to the local community (PSNI representative - Operational).

Police officers reported a sense of frustration and anger within communities with the criminal justice system and more specifically sentencing. There were concerns from community groups around the lack of consistency in punishments:

I could name you five or six people who have went to the PPS with twenty different referrals, but they might only be prosecuted on two or three…it is very frustrating for the police, but also the people on the ground who have reported these perpetrators (PSNI representative - Operational).

It was interesting to note that the lack of prosecutions, or more importantly the lack of communication and information surrounding why particular cases are not prosecuted, has a detrimental impact on the ability of the police to exercise their roles and responsibilities. A key tenet of policing is the sharing of information. Essentially the police cannot deliver policing without the support and engagement of the community. According to one officer, members of the public were reluctant to report crimes, or provide information on specific incidents, because there was an assumption that the courts would not deal with the perpetrator in a punitive manner. One respondent recalled a conversation with a victim of crime:

What's the point of me giving information cause there is the guy back on the street again, back doing whatever he wants...back to intimidate me (PSNI representative - Operational).

One further development that was mentioned arising from the lack of consistency in prosecutions and sentences relates to the perception that the police are recruiting informers or 'touts'. According to police officers, in some cases members of the public have accused the police of reducing charges in return for information. There was no evidence to support this, but historically the use of informers who originally engaged in petty crime has been widespread (Helsinki Watch, 1993), and members of the public who see the lack of prosecutions have assumed that the police continue to recruit.

There continues to be a degree of mystery surrounding the PPS and the rationale employed for prosecuting individuals. Unfortunately as one officer has summarised:

The police are seen as being the criminal justice system and if these people get off with light sentences the police are often blamed (PSNI representative - Strategic).

In this new dispensation of policing, encouraging the community to both participate and actively engage in the sharing of information is crucial if the police are to fulfill their roles and responsibilities. However, the current inconsistencies surrounding prosecutions and sentences, along with the lack of sharing of information or explanation of decision-making, has the potential to damage both the image of the PSNI and the wider criminal justice system.

Future of policing

Each of the officers was asked to provide their vision for the future of policing in Northern Ireland. As discussions with representatives from the Northern Ireland Policing Board revealed there is great deal of international interest in the development of policing in Northern Ireland. One police officer felt it was important to reflect on the positive successes achieved in relation to policing in the last decade, and the pride the organisation had in sharing their experience with other police services:

A lot of people are looking for our expertise, we have police officers who are travelling the world showing different jurisdictions what we are doing (PSNI representative - Strategic).

Discussions also focused on the appearance of police stations and the potential for them to be made more aesthetically pleasing. It was anticipated that in the future, and depending on the security situation, the 'softening' of the police stations was something that all police officers would welcome:

We are working towards defortifying the police stations…but it is a long process. Look at Coleraine and Newcastle, such a difference, again the security situation impacts on this process (PSNI representative - Strategic).

There was also a view that overall the organisation had become very bureaucratic, and there was a danger that it could become entrenched with procedures, forms and a paranoia to be accountable. On the other hand, one officer noted that, in response to the legacy of the past and the accusations made against policing, being open and accountable is necessary:

I think that one of our greatest defences now is that we are very transparent (PSNI representative - Strategic).

This is the only way to develop the confidence for communities from both Loyalist and Republican areas to engage openly with the police. It is a two way process, the police cannot deliver on their roles and responsibilities without the support and participation of local communities, and local communities cannot address issues of concern around crime and community safety without the resources, knowledge and skills of the police.

One officer summed it up best when they talked about contemporary policing within the context of policing in the last thirty years. There have been so many significant changes, and there will continue to be improvements:

There have been so many improvements in recent years. After the ceasefires we were walking around with the army with up to sixteen squaddies, from then it went to about six with us on the beat, now it is just a couple of officers (PSNI representative - Operational).

On reflection the future of policing will be shaped by the strength of the relationships cultivated by the police at the community level, and the degree of confidence the community has in working in partnership with the police to address their issues of community safety and crime.

Summary

The police have undergone a number of structural, operational and more importantly organisational changes in the last decade. Considering their role throughout the conflict and the injuries and loss of life experienced by the police it has proved an emotive and sensitive period in their history. However, there was an acknowledgement that the police had to change and adapt to the new social and political climate evident within Northern Ireland. Post-ceasefire policing is very different to policing during the conflict. There is a stronger emphasis on building and sustaining relationships and forging new partnerships with communities and different statutory agencies. However, there was also a realisation that this was to take place within the context of decreasing resources, increased community expectations, and continued threats and attacks from dissident Republicans and elements from within Loyalist communities.

It was apparent that the police recognised the need to develop positive working partnerships in the community. They understood the importance of the existing community-based initiatives and programmes and these appeared compatible with the workings of the formal criminal justice system. However, these partnerships were relatively new and still in their infancy. The boundaries between the community's ownership of community safety programmes and initiatives and the role of the PSNI has yet to be established or more importantly tested. What is clear is that there is a realisation from the police that they alone do not hold the key to addressing criminality and anti-social behaviour. Instead a multi-agency approach with strong community participation is necessary for dealing and responding to these incidents.

There was a degree of criticism of the DPPs and the overall impact they had in supporting the police. There was some confusion around the role of DPPs and whether their emphasis was on consultation with communities, facilitation between communities and the police, or monitoring the police against their policing plans. Generally, the police welcomed the rationale for implementing DPPs but ultimately indicated that their true potential was being restricted because of public apathy towards them. It was noted that since Sinn Féin had taken their places on the DPP that attendance at several public meetings had increased, but again their contribution to local policing issues had yet to be evaluated.

The new relationships with the Republican community were welcomed, although it was noted the potential impact this community would have on existing capacity and resources. The police often referred to the lack of resources and there was a hint of hesitancy from officers about meeting these communities' expectations while their numbers continue to decrease. Discussions on the implementation and delivery of community policing received mixed responses. It became apparent that at a strategic level it was not receiving enough support or direction. Communities were keen for engagement and discussions to take place, but it appeared that organisationally community policing was too often sacrificed for more measurable targets.

7. District Policing Partnerships

The following section documents the main findings from discussions with independent members of District Policing Partnerships along with Northern Ireland Policing Board Members.

District Policing Partnerships (DPPs) are a partnership between the district councillors and representatives of the local community for the purpose of monitoring the effectiveness of policing in that local area. There are nineteen members of a DPP, ten of whom are from political parties, and nine are independent members. There are twenty-six DPPs in Northern Ireland that reflect the number of district council areas. DPPs are responsible for consulting and engaging with communities in relation to developing local policing plans; monitoring the performance of the police in carrying out the policing plan; and acting as a general forum for discussion and consultation on local matters impacting on the policing of the district. The DPPs were reconstituted in April 2008 with elected members of Sinn Féin finally taking their places on the partnerships.

The **Northern Ireland Policing Board (NIPB),** established in 2001, is an independent public body made up of nineteen members, ten of whom are from political parties and nine are independent members. The key role of the Board is to hold the Chief Constable to account; oversee complaints against senior police officers; secure an effective and efficient local police service; consult widely with local people about the policing of their area; establish police priorities and targets for police performance; and monitor everything the police do and how well they perform against targets set by the Board.

A number of themes emerged from the discussions with members of the NIPB along with elected and independent members of the DPP in Belfast that have been outlined below. As part of the research the author also attended four public DPP meetings in November 2007. These meetings took place in North, South, East and West Belfast. The meeting in West Belfast was the first public DPP meeting involving Sinn Féin as active participants and was symbolically held in a leisure centre off the Falls Road.

These meetings provided the author with an opportunity to experience first hand the level of community interest in the DPPs, along with the types of issues and concerns residents were raising with their local police.

The role of a DPP

There was a general consensus from both independent and elected members that the concept of the DPPs was viewed as positive in developing relationships between local communities and the police, and to further instil confidence in the new policing structures that had been developed following the Patten Report:

I think that it is a positive move to allow politicians and lay people to engage directly with the police on their own local issues (DPP Independent).

One respondent was quick to acknowledge the impact of the DPPs and how they were instrumental in facilitating communication and dialogue between local communities and the police:

The position of being on the DPP has meant that I have been able to react positively to community disputes and issues that have the potential to escalate…I have brokered talks between the police and local community which has addressed their concerns and prevented rumour-mongering (DPP Independent).

Initial discussions revealed that there were a number of elements linked to the DPP. One related to actual members of DPPs and their perceived roles and duties, while the second focused on the general public's perception and knowledge of DPPs. According to a number of interviewees there was often a degree of confusion as to their role in their partnership between facilitating relationships between the police and local communities, and on the other hand holding the police to account:

There are DPP members who don't even see their role as developing engagement…they expect the management staff to go out and consult with groups, but that's not their role (DPP Independent).

Discussions revealed that the concept of 'community consultation' caused a degree of difficulty in that different members interpreted it in very different ways. There were some who indicated that as there were political representatives on the partnership, then they automatically represented the views of the community. Other independent members were of the persuasion that it was the responsibility of the DPP to go into the community, engage and debate with local residents and provide a service for people to discuss their issues and concerns around policing. Their major concern centred on who were the appropriate people to consult with:

It is the members of the DPPs responsibility to be out engaging with, and speaking with communities, but the difficulty I suppose from a DPP point of view is who are the people that you are supposed to consult with? (DPP Independent).

There was also a degree of frustration from one interviewee surrounding the actual impact DPP members were having in engaging with local communities. It was implied that DPPs conduct 'tick box' exercises set down by the NIPB, but in reality these do very little to monitor the effectiveness the DPPs are having in relation to facilitating relationships between local communities and the police:

A number of the structures at the moment are centred around producing a consultation report; an annual report; holding four meetings per year…now you can do all those things, but when it comes to 'did each individual member go out and knock on doors, go out to community centres and give presentations, talk to people, introduce themselves as a DPP member and try and get people to understand what their role is…then the answer would be no' (DPP Independent).

Questions were raised as to the monitoring of DPPs and whether the NIPB were aware of the issues/concerns around the lack of involvement of certain individual members in actively engaging with communities around policing. The current monitoring of DPPs was criticised along with a perceived distancing between DPPs and the NIPB:

The NI Policing Board know that we have members who aren't fulfilling that (aspect of engaging with communities) but they are not rectifying it…and the structures that they have at the moment around monitoring are so weak that there is no control of them (DPP Independent).

It should be noted that all of the interviewees provided examples of community engagement and initiatives where there was facilitation between the police and the community. These included incidents where members attended workshops with youth providers and organisations that supported older members of the community. Other instances that were recalled included DPP members that had attended community functions and school events and highlighted the role of the DPP and encouraged communities to develop positive relationships with the police.

However, there was a degree of frustration from some independent members around the productivity and commitment of elected members in relation to consulting with the community. The reality according to a number of Independent members was that elected members were often reluctant to engage in community initiatives or participate in programmes aimed at promoting the roles and responsibilities of the DPP. There was no apparent reason attributed for this lack of commitment expressed by elected members, and it is important not to generalise, but the independent members' experiences were ones of disengagement.

Public perceptions of DPPs

There was a strongly held view from a number of interviewees that the public were largely unaware of the DPPs and their position within the context of policing and justice:

A lot of young people probably don't even know that the DPP exists, and who they are, and what they are supposed to be doing (DPP Independent).

It was argued that the NIPB point to independent surveys highlighting the large percentage of people who claim to know and understand what is meant by a DPP. The most recent NIPB survey indicated that 76 per cent of respondents had heard of DPPs (NIPB, 2008). However, several interviewees disagreed and felt that only a minority of the public understood their role, and more importantly, how to access them. Interestingly, Hamilton et al (2003) in a survey of over one thousand young people concluded that 77 per cent had not heard of a DPP. Although this research was conducted five years ago, it was not a postal survey and highlights the significant apathy shown by young people to DPPs. This along with anecdotal evidence led many to indicate that there needed to be more done to draw attention to their role:

There needs to be a more concerted effort to inform the public of our role and the benefits we can offer in relation to facilitating relationships between the police and community (DPP Elected member).

Elected and independent members noted that they constantly had to explain their role and position in relation to policing to members of the public. There was confusion from communities as to the powers associated with the DPP, with a number of respondents recalling incidents where they were mistaken for both being members of the police and the Police Ombudsman's Office.

Member attendance

A common theme from independent DPP members focused on the

attendance rates of those members from a political party. There was a general consensus that a number of political members had poor attendance records at both public and private meetings. Furthermore, on the occasions that they did attend meetings, some stayed for a limited time and then left:

There are supposed to be trigger points that notify when attendance is poor...last year there was one political member attended something like one out of twenty meetings...but they are still on the DPP, something is not working (DPP Independent).

A further independent member noted that on occasions there was a sense that the elected members, regardless of their political background, would take the side of fellow politicians against independent members. There was a chasm between elected and independents on different topics:

There was a sense that they resented us (independent members) being on the DPPs. That we were not intelligent enough, or couldn't contribute positively to debates (DPP Independent).

Representatives from the NI Policing Board were aware of this issue and noted that:

Attendance of members is something that we are very aware of; we have received records from DPP managers and it is something that we aim to address (Policing Board).

Table 2 highlights the percentage of public and private meetings attended by both elected and independent members of the Belfast Partnership. They clearly show that there is a significant difference between members, with independents attending at least twice as many meetings as their elected counterparts.

Table 2 Belfast DPP Members Attendance at Meetings in Public and Private Meetings of the Principal Partnership and its Four Sub-Groups 2005-2007

	2005-2006	2006-2007
Elected Members	33%	41%
Independent Members	82%	80%

One respondent noted that although attendance was important it was also crucial that those members that were present at meetings actively contributed:

There was one member who attended every single meeting, they didn't speak, they didn't contribute, they didn't monitor or consult, what use is that? (DPP Independent).

There is no doubting the discrepancy in attendance figures between elected and independent members in the Belfast DPP. According to independent members this apparent level of commitment from elected members to the process was both frustrating and illustrated a lack of engagement in the policing debate. This was one of the major criticisms from independent members because several had expected more from the elected members. They were under the impression that they had the skills, capacity and experience to challenge the police, stimulate community interest in policing issues and offer guidance to the independents. However, this was not the case and they found themselves on numerous sub-groups and conducting substantial pieces of DPP work, with little support from political representatives.

Sinn Fein Participation

Discussions turned to the impact of Sinn Féin taking their places on the DPPs and NIPB. Their arrival was welcomed, and it was anticipated that they would bring a fresh impetus to the public and private meetings:

Of course they will question more, ask questions…as a result existing members will have to challenge more. It will be interesting to take the policing debate into communities that have never engaged formally with the police (DPP Independent).

It was also interesting to note that other interviewees maintained that although Sinn Féin were now engaged in the policing debate, their participation would not guarantee the future safety of police or DPP members. They acknowledged that there remained a calculated threat from dissident Republicans who would continue to attempt to derail the political stability through attacks against elements of the criminal justice system:

Sinn Féin is on board and there are still incidents of DPPs being threatened, there are still security risks, the police are still being targeted…so anybody who thought that the minute Sinn Féin came on board that all of that was going to stop was living in cloud cuckoo land (DPP Independent).

Along with the recognition of Sinn Féin's movement in relation to policing, there was a degree of caution with respect to Loyalist communities. One interviewee realised the benefits of having Sinn Féin within the policing debate, influencing policy and questioning decisions for all communities. However, they were concerned that as Republican communities would grow and possibly embrace new programmes and initiatives around policing and community safety, Loyalist communities would instead regress, become more insular and refrain from participating or establishing new relationships with police and criminal justice organisations:

It is remarkable that they (Republicans) have come so far…within the next two years I think that you are going to see a very confident Republican community dealing with policing…my worry is that Loyalist communities will not participate in the same way (DPP Independent).

There was general agreement that at this stage assessing the impact of Sinn Féin officially engaging and participating with the criminal justice system would prove difficult. Only a couple of months had passed, and the true test could only be examined after at least a year.

Violence, intimidation and threats

Discussions centred on the potential dangers associated with being a member of a DPP, and whether this would be an influence in continuing to engage and work within the criminal justice system. Independent and elected members of DPPs have in the past been threatened for their involvement in policing issues. A number of members have been intimidated, received bullets in the post and had property damaged. These incidents have for the most part been associated with either mainstream or dissident Republicans (BBC News, 15.09.03). However, Loyalists have also been involved in issuing threats, usually in association with parading disputes (BBC News, 19.06.04). It was noted that in the last five years threats against members of DPPs had significantly diminished. One interviewee felt this was the result of stability in the criminal justice system, and the advent of Sinn Féin 'signing up to policing'.

There continue to be areas within Northern Ireland that do not wish to engage, or develop meaningful relationships, with the police or the DPPs. One such area, the Markets in South Belfast, was the location for a DPP meeting on 28th November 2007. The meeting was unable to proceed as a result of a demonstration in the community centre that was to be the venue for the public meeting (BBC News, 20.11.07). There were heated discussions between members of the community and the DPP, with the demonstrators indicating that the meeting was being forced upon them without prior consultation. It was interesting to note that a senior Sinn Féin MLA in attendance was continually heckled and called a traitor. This incident illustrated the deep resentment among some within the Republican community to Sinn Féin's engagement with the police and the criminal justice system. The episode also provided an illustration of the community's negative perceptions of the police, with shouts of 'SS RUC' and 'Loyalist death squads' echoing around the centre. It is important to note that it was difficult to determine whether these protestors were representative of the entire local community. However, discussions with one demonstrator indicated that this group felt let down by Sinn Féin, and ostracised from the wider Republican community because they continued to reject existing state forces.

Public meetings

A significant part of the discussions examined the current method of engaging local communities through public meetings. There were mixed responses as to whether they were the most practical and encouraging system of involving the public in the workings of the DPP. A number of interviewees were of the view that the meetings were very adversarial, enshrined in procedures and were not flexible enough to address the needs of local communities, who often wanted to raise very specific concerns:

I am not too sure that the mechanisms employed through the current DPPs in terms of having public meetings, are the proper methods to encourage local people to come along and air their views (DPP Independent).

However, it became apparent that for some DPP members, the meetings should be more strategic and not become 'talking shops' for local residents who see the public meetings as an opportunity to criticise the police. It was clear that there was a delicate balance between dealing with local community-based issues and wider issues of policing in general:

They should not focus on the micro-issues…and provide a platform for individuals to lambast the police for their lack of response to a particular incident (DPP Independent).

There was a general consensus that public meetings had not been well attended. There had been numerous occasions that meetings throughout Northern Ireland involved no members of the public attending. According to the Belfast Telegraph (12.06.07) between 2003 and 2006 there were eleven meetings without a single member of the public in attendance. On the other hand, if there was a significant issue, this often provided the catalyst for large attendances. Significantly, these issues often referred to parading disputes. It was suggested that although public meetings were not overly well attended, the fact that they were taking place was a measure of their success, they provided an opportunity to monitor and hold the police to account in a safe and transparent manner.

It was noted on a number of occasions that topics around policing and criminal justice can be extremely boring to people who have either no interest in the subject matter or have no grievances with the police, and therefore significant turnouts at public meetings should not be expected. It was interesting to note that several interviewees felt that now Sinn Féin were part of the DPPs that larger numbers would attend the public meetings:

Sinn Féin have come on board they're bringing a section of the community that were not engaging with policing previously (DPP Independent).

This was evident at the recent DPP meeting in West Belfast in November 2007 (An Phoblacht, 06.12.07). This was the first DPP meeting held on the Falls Road that involved the local community and representatives from the local police district. Although there was a small peaceful protest outside the meeting by the Irish Republican Socialist Party the meeting was attended by approximately 200 local residents, and passed off without incident. In recent months public demonstrations against DPP public meetings have significantly diminished.

PSNI

A further development was the relationship between the DPP and the police. For the most part interviewees indicated that this was positive and that the police were more than willing to provide information, respond to specific queries and establish working relationships. However, there were those who felt the police were simply participating in a 'tick box' exercise and participating because they had to, not because they wanted to or could see any benefits:

The police I do not think have engaged sufficiently with DPPs…they have bypassed them…they realise that due to legislation that they have to engage with them but only cause they have to (DPP Independent).

There was a perception that the police often viewed the DPPs as an afterthought, and did not see them as having an integral role in developing and facilitating partnerships within the community. To some extent this was not viewed as a direct criticism of the police, but more of government and the NIPB. The role of the DPP was not simply to hold the police to account and monitor their actions. The respondents felt that DPPs had a unique opportunity to complement the work of the police, develop new links into the community, and create an environment where policing could be debated in an open and transparent manner. However, they maintained that this view was not being reciprocated by the police:

If tomorrow there's a new piece of legislation that said the police had to meet say a women's group four times a year, then they would build it into their plans…but they are not going to change how they conduct their job (DPP Independent).

This concern of the level of commitment from the police to the DPPs was countered by other interviewees who recognised the significant contribution that the police had made in both making themselves more accountable and building partnerships with specific hard to reach groups.

Managing community expectations

One interesting finding centred around the idea of having to educate communities about the role of the police. According to a number of interviewees there was limited knowledge on the powers and resources of the police. Many, especially those from Nationalist/Republican communities had never experienced policing within a 'normal' context therefore they had specific perceptions and expectations of the criminal justice system. A large number of communities had been governed by paramilitary organisations, and as such had lived within the context of an informal justice system. The realities of the formal system are very different:

You now have communities that are having to deal with issues around drug dealers and anti-social behaviour…it is very different how policing and our judicial system can deal with those people in comparison to a paramilitary coming round, threatening and putting a gun to someone's kneecap…Communities are going to get frustrated…they are going to expect that as soon as they report someone for breaking the law that the police are going to come down, lift them, then arrest them and eventually they will go to court, but that doesn't happen (DPP Independent).

The discussions revealed that one key legacy of the conflict was an expectancy that the police would deliver and respond to every individual incident. Security budgets and resources had been significantly higher than in England and Wales, which meant that previously the police were in a position to respond to the majority of call-outs. However, since the reform of the policing and criminal justice systems there has been a considerable decrease in the numbers of police officers and other security personnel:

There used to be more people to deliver the service, this has raised expectations...people remember the visible police presence ten years ago, that just don't exist anymore (DPP Independent).

It became apparent that there was an onus on all areas of the criminal justice system to inform communities of the realities of policing. Interviewees noted that through their discussions with community groups and local residents there was a large degree of anger and frustration with the local police. There were complaints around response times, attitudes at crime scenes and a general sense of disengagement with the entire criminal justice system:

I think under the old policing system we were spoiled and we expected the police to respond to every incident, they might not have been able to do anything but the fact was they came...now they are having to prioritise call-outs and our expectations are greater I think than the police can deliver on (DPP Independent)

Interestingly respondents were asked whether they felt communities in the future may request a return to the times when paramilitary type organisations would administer quick and responsive justice. There was a general consensus that this was not something that was currently being voiced in the communities, but they could not discount a change in attitudes in the future.

Role of the Criminal Justice System

There were a number of points raised by interviewees around the role of the judiciary, with specific attention placed on the sentencing of offenders. In recent years the media have been quick to highlight lenient sentencing and minimal bail conditions for repeat offenders. According to one interviewee the public were associating the wider criminal justice system with the police, and were subsequently reflecting any frustration or anger they had with prosecuting or sentencing upon them:

There is a perception that the judiciary is not doing enough…while you have the police performing their duties and doing their job, if they are going to be let down by the judiciary, it will reflect badly on the police (DPP Independent).

This was a recurring theme throughout the discussions with the PPS and other elements of the criminal justice system such as the Prison Service and the judiciary coming under strong criticism. In part this was a result of a lack of knowledge or information surrounding the decision-making process in relation to the prosecuting and/or sentencing of offenders. The general public felt distant and unattached with these sections of the criminal justice system:

Even when the police do get them, they still have the PPS deciding to reject files and not to prosecute…or when they do they get to court and the judge gives someone a slap on the wrist and they are back out laughing at the community (DPP Elected).

In recent months DPP members had been inundated with queries around the sentencing of offenders. According to several interviewees there was a recognisable need to develop stronger relationships between the different agencies of the criminal justice system and possibly facilitate discussions within the community that highlight the roles and responsibilities of each particular agency.

Community Safety Partnerships

Interviewees were asked whether they felt that there was replication around roles and responsibilities between DPPs and Community Safety Partnerships (CSP.). There was a general consensus that within the context of policing and community safety there was merit in amalgamating both partnerships. Currently, the DPPs have limited resources to fund programmes around developing partnerships between the community and the police. However, Community Safety Partnerships have a significantly larger budget for these types of initiatives:

It's OK asking the DPP to engage with the police and communities in the prevention of crime…but you need to put the resources in…our budget compared to Community Safety is peanuts (DPP representative).

Discussions with a Community Safety Partnership representative indicated that it was not impossible for the two partnerships to potentially merge in the future, as it did not make sense for both bodies to have similar roles and responsibilities leading to incidents of replication. The Crime

Reduction Partnerships in England were highlighted as a possible model for the future amalgamation of the partnerships to adopt. It is interesting to note that the Review of the Criminal Justice System in Northern Ireland (2000) concluded that as policing was an important aspect of community safety then DPPs and CSPs should be replaced with single Community Safety and Policing Partnerships, chaired by local authority elected members. However, this recommendation was not accepted and a dual system of partnerships was adopted.

Community relationships

Attempts were made to gain an understanding of the different methods that could potentially facilitate relationships between the police and the community. All of the interviewees indicated support for Community Police Support Officers (similar to those implemented in England and Wales from 2003) they perceived them as an extra resource to support the police in developing partnerships with the community. They were viewed as complementary to the regular police service:

The key with introducing them in Northern Ireland is making sure that they are actually building up contacts in the local community…helping local groups, engaging and supporting the regular police officers (DPP Independent).

The NI Policing Board acknowledged that there was willingness to implement CPSOs, however resource issues have continued to hinder their development within Northern Ireland. The Board points to their possible future role in supporting the police, establishing links within communities and providing a high visibility and reassurance to communities using a problem-solving approach to tackling quality of life issues. It is interesting to note that recent media attention has indicated that CPSOs will not be implemented in Northern Ireland for the foreseeable future due to a shortfall in the policing budget (Belfast Telegraph 19.05.08).

The NIPB reiterated the importance of developing relationships between the police and communities. They illustrated this by discussing an innovative idea around implementing community policing within a small town setting (NIPB, 07.12.07), the idea being that the local police would occupy an agreed amount of space in a new community centre to provide local policing in that area. It was envisaged that the police could develop partnerships and become an integral part of the local community. The idea has been driven by the local community, and involves a partnership with the police and the NIPB.

The NIPB also pointed out the development of their Community Engagement Strategy (2008) with the aims of developing new relationships with particular hard to reach groups and highlighting the role of the Board. The Strategy headed up by the Sinn Féin MLA Alex Maskey is conducting a number of consultations and discussion groups with young people, minority ethnic groups, older people and lesbian and gay, bisexual, and transgender groups. Furthermore, it is anticipated that through engagement they will be in a position to enhance the influence they have over communities on policing, and provide the Board with an opportunity to explore the specific needs of the community.

One area that several interviewees felt may inhibit developing partnerships with the community centred on the current structure and appearance of police stations. They were of the opinion that they did not encourage people to actively engage with the police, even in non-policing matters. As one respondent commented on their local police station:

It is physically intimidating. There is nothing that is going to make you go in casually…everything is to keep you out of it. People are not going to simply walk in and pass on information (DPP Independent).

According to the NIPB the 'softening' of police stations is a particular area that they have been examining, and point to examples such as Coleraine and Newcastle where existing police stations have been made more aesthetically pleasing. It was also noted that the security situation dictates the time frame for reducing the security barricades at police stations, and while there is a credible threat from dissident Republicans (Belfast Telegraph 07.02.08), the organisation has a duty of care to its officers. Interestingly the final report from the Office of the Oversight Commission, which was responsible for assessing whether the recommendations from the Patten Report had been implemented, concluded that although the softening of police stations and the removal of fortifications had begun it was occurring at a very slow pace (Office of the Oversight Commissioner, Report 19, 2007).

Summary

The DPP members, both independent and elected, highlighted the potential positive role that the partnerships could have in relation to developing relationships between the police and local communities. However, there was an acknowledgement that the majority of the general public were unsure of the roles and responsibilities of a DPP member. This was reflected in the poor attendance at the majority of public meetings. There had been recorded instances where no members of the public attended the meetings.

Independent members noted that it was the responsibility of DPPs to essentially inform the public of their role, and facilitate engagement with the police. There was a degree of criticism from several members around the amount of engagement and interaction with communities that DPPs actually participated in. There were a number of examples of good practice mentioned but it became apparent that engagement and facilitating relationship building between the public and police was not viewed as a crucial element of the DPPs by a number of members.

A further criticism of the DPPs from the independent members centred on the attendance and contribution of a number of elected representatives of the partnerships. There was a general consensus that they were not supporting the process or contributing in a positive and meaningful manner. Questions were raised as to the role of the NIPB in managing and monitoring the roles of the DPPs. There did not appear to be adequate monitoring of members' attendance at public and private meetings. Nor were there appropriate mechanisms in place to assess the impact DPPs were having in both monitoring the PSNI at a local level, but more importantly facilitating relationships between the community and the police. Several members also questioned the willingness of the PSNI to engage with DPPs. A number of members had experiences where the police appeared not to be interested in the benefits of DPPs and viewed them as a hindrance and an obstacle to policing.

8. Discussion

The research has provided the opportunity to offer a comprehensive account of Republican and Loyalist communities' and PSNI's experiences of the new dispensation of policing in this post-conflict society. We are eighteen months into this era, and it is clear that there are a number of issues and concerns prevalent within both communities and the PSNI. The following section will attempt to draw out the main implications that emerged from the discussions with Loyalists, Republicans and the PSNI and provide an analysis of the future direction of policing within the current climate. From the outset the findings revealed the deep-rooted sensitivities that continue to surround the area of policing and justice. However, it was evident that all of the main protagonists recognised both the symbolic and practical benefits of having a police service that is endorsed by all of the political parties and is acceptable to the majority of local communities. Ten years after the signing of the Agreement there was a realisation that the acceptance and legitimisation of the policing service was a significant event within the context of the Troubles.

Key components

In analysing the research findings it became apparent that there are three key elements responsible for the successful implementation of the community policing programme. Republicans, Loyalists and the police have all undergone significant changes in recent years in adapting to a new social and political environment. The Republican community, Loyalist community and PSNI were the central figures during this new chapter for policing and justice in Northern Ireland. They have each viewed and internalised the policing reform process in very different ways. Furthermore, the process of reform and its subsequent impact has been extremely difficult for sections within each of these groups to take on board. However, although each of the groups has approached the policing and justice debate very differently there appears to be one underlying factor that has been consistent within each of the groups, namely the legacy of the past. Memories, attitudes, perceptions and identities in relation to policing were governed very much by the Troubles, and as a result each group interpreted policing and what it represented very differently.

PSNI

The lead agency in the implementation of a successful community policing programme is the PSNI. The policing structures in Northern

Ireland have undergone monumental changes in the last decade. However, it is important to note that police reform is not a concept simply synomonous with Northern Ireland. There are a number of examples of countries reforming their policing structures. These included the Balkans as a result of ethnic conflict (Peake, 2004); South Africa as part of the political and social reform process (Brewer, 1994); and Belgium after a number of scandals that highlighted organisational incompetence (Maesschalck, 2002).

With respect to Northern Ireland there has been a general consensus that the police reform process has been a success. Delegations from numerous jurisdictions throughout the world have attended briefings in Northern Ireland outlining the significant changes that emerged from the reform process. Specific attention is constantly placed on the transparency of the organisation and the comprehensive accountability mechanisms to monitor the delivery of its roles and responsibilities. The reform process along with the successful implementation of these changes in a transitional society emerging from thirty years of violence cannot be understated. Several countries have attempted processes of police transformation and failed, including post-communist Russia (Pustintsev, 2000); Hungary and Lithuania (Koci, 1998); and Bosnia-Herzegovina (Dominique, 2003).

The discussions with the PSNI representatives were very illuminating and touched on the difficulties that many within the organisation had during the reform process. They highlighted the complex nature of policing along with the problems they have encountered attempting to meet the communities' expectations against a backdrop of reduced capacity and resources, with increased budget cuts. The whole concept of community policing was discussed with mixed views on its impact and more importantly its position within the strategic framework of the PSNI. Those engaging in community policing recognised the benefits of developing partnerships with local groups and maintaining an environment where observing and engaging with the police was a normal community activity. However, there was also a degree of concern as to how much support at the higher levels of the organisation community policing was receiving. Similar to any major corporation the PSNI is measured on productivity and results. Figures, percentages and performance ratings dictate policing agendas and influence the allocation of resources and unfortunately the successes attributed to community policing are very difficult to measure.

There did not appear to be any difference in how the PSNI engaged with Republican or Loyalist communities. There was a concern from dissident threats in certain Republican areas, but this was not viewed as a significant factor in limiting the police's ability to deliver a positive service. There was a realisation that existing community safety programmes at the local level had proved successful in facilitating relationships. Furthermore, there did not appear to be reluctance from the PSNI to establishing working partnerships with ex-combatants. There were emotional and sensitive issues associated with this element of policing, but it was widely recognised that these individuals continued to have a degree of support and influence within their respective communities. It was crucial to include these individuals and groups in policing initiatives and programmes so that the wider community witnessed the engagement and followed their lead.

The threat from dissidents was noted as a factor in the ability of the PSNI to provide a more 'normalised' sense of policing in relation to their uniform, transport and the appearance of police stations. It has been recognised that attempts have been made to visually soften some stations, remove body armour and provide bicycles and high visibility cars. However, these improvements were very much dictated by the security threat. It was also noted that many of these changes to policing were more likely to occur in more affluent, middle class areas of Northern Ireland and not in Loyalist and Republican working class areas.

Republican community

Discussions with members of the Republican community focused on two central themes. Firstly, the negative perceptions of policing, the persecutions experienced by their community and the discriminatory police practice in operation during the Troubles. The second theme was more complex and centred on the symbolic meaning of Republicans endorsing a police service under a devolved government in Northern Ireland. Historically, the community has been loathe to engage with the police as a result of negative experiences, community pressure or fear from the paramilitaries. This created a vacuum of policing and justice that was filled by Republican paramilitaries and more recently by community-based initiatives and restorative justice programmes.

These projects and organisations have been at the forefront in facilitating relationships and creating partnerships between the local community and the PSNI in the last eighteen months. Although communities recognised the need for policing, the decision from Sinn Féin to endorse the PSNI was a seismic shift within Republicanism. From the outset communities required support and confidence-building measures to realise that engagement with the PSNI was no longer viewed as 'touting' or collaborating with the enemy.

This brings me on to the second theme that referred to the ideological and political difficulties that a number of Republicans had with Sinn Féin's participation in the policing and justice structures. A central tenet of Republican ideology was the hostility towards the British state, with specific attention placed on the mechanisms of social control, and particularly the police. Therefore, an acceptance of the policing structures, while Northern Ireland remained part of the United Kingdom and Westminister continued to administer control, contradicted everything that Republicans had campaigned against throughout the conflict. Sinn Féin have to be commended for the manner in which they decided upon recognising the legitimacy of the PSNI without fracturing the Republican community.

It has been suggested that Sinn Féin's significant shift in policy was aided by the community's demand for a responsive police service. There was no doubt that working class communities had suffered from violent crime, anti-social behaviour, and a rise in the fear of crime in the years between the paramilitary ceasefires and Sinn Féin's endorsement of the PSNI. Therefore, there was an acceptance that a formal police service was their only opportunity to address the issues and concerns around criminality and community safety.

According to the research findings, although there was 'an eagerness from communities for policing' and there was a sense of novelty around police engagement, it was felt that this would not last forever. There currently is a honeymoon period involving the PSNI and the Republican community. In most cases the community are receptive to different initiatives, are keen to develop partnerships and work alongside the PSNI. However, it was apparent that at some stage, if the community's expectations are not being met and concerns continue around the service delivery of policing, then the honeymoon period could end. There was a strong view that now was the time for the PSNI to invest resources and capacity in establishing partnerships with the Republican community.

Depending on how you analyse it, either the Republican journey on policing has come to an end, or is only beginning. No longer are they on the outside challenging and criticising yet providing no suitable and practical alternative. They are now central to the policing debate, visible by their presence on the Northern Ireland Policing Board and the District Policing Partnerships. There have been criticisms from some elements of the Republican community that Sinn Féin have not shown enough leadership or provided support at a grass roots level. There was some evidence to support this, but it was also clear that existing community and restorative justice groups have shown guidance and facilitated engagement between the community and the police. One becomes aware of how far we have come as a society in such a brief time when Republican newspapers such as the Andersonstown News have regular features titled 'Crime Log – police assistance needed' and carry recruitment advertisements for the PSNI.

At the strategic echelons of Republicanism the devolution of policing and justice is crucial for the justification of their endorsement of the PSNI. However, on a practical level local communities are focused more on the issues of police response times, visible policing, and the sentencing of repeat offenders. At the time of writing there is no confirmation when the policing and justice powers will be devolved to the Stormont Assembly. Ironically, there is the potential for policing to become politicised once more, as the two dominant political parties, the DUP and Sinn Féin, attempt to use the transfer of policing and justice as a bargaining chip within the context of other political decisions such as the Irish Language Act, the abolition of the transfer test and water charges.

Loyalist community

In certain sections of Northern Ireland there is a stereotypical view that Loyalists have a strong affiliation with the policing structures. The findings from the research indicate that this could not be further from the truth. There is a high level of dissatisfaction with the police and issues around association, identity and the development of positive working partnerships continue to dominate the relationship between the Loyalist community and the PSNI. There are a number of complex dynamics evident within Loyalist communities that go some way to provide an understanding of their relationship with the police.

One important concern was the apparent lack of political support or leadership within Loyalist communities in relation to policing compared to the role of Sinn Féin in Republican areas. Loyalist communities were at a significant disadvantage, with limited support at a strategic level for policing and community safety issues. For several years, paramilitary organisations such as the UDA and UVF kept a degree of control over the Loyalist communities, in a sense there was no need for political support within the communities as the paramilitaries controlled much of the community infrastructure and provided forms of community policing and justice. However, in recent years Loyalist paramilitaries have distanced themselves from forms of social control and violence. They have acknowledged that the conflict is over and encouraged the communities to engage with and use the PSNI (www.bbc.co.uk/ni, 12.12.07). There is now a vacuum with no political representatives in a position to replace the paramilitaries and champion the needs of the working class Loyalist communities.

Loyalist communities have adapted to this lack of support and similarly Republican communities have attempted to encourage debate and engagement from the bottom up. Communities themselves have taken the initiative and developed conversations at the grass roots level in the hope of influencing those in more strategic positions. They have looked at the membership of District Policing Partnerships, but have been unable to identify with individual members, who they believe are not in a position to relate to the needs and concerns of working class communities. A major frustration for these communities is the fact that the government and other statutory agencies continue to take for granted the idea that there is a positive relationship between Loyalists and the PSNI, and instead focus attention, resources and encouragement on developing sustainable relationships between Republicans and the PSNI. The reality is very different, reporting crime in some cases is still seen as 'touting', paramilitaries continue to exert control and there is a clear and present view that policing is there to coerce and punish rather than serve and protect.

Areas of commonality

Regardless of their community background it was clear that Loyalist and Republican working class communities find it extremely difficult to identify with policing. The PSNI and organisations such as the DPPs were viewed as middle class institutions without the knowledge or understanding to comprehend the issues prevalent within working class communities. There was a strong suspicion that the police were isolated from the key concerns of these communities. It was no longer about the discrimination of Protestants or Catholics, and a police service for one community over another. The underlying issues were class-based and concerned the delivery of a service that appeared to favour middle class over working class. Communities were distinguishing not between the differences in policing the Falls and Shankill, but instead the differences in response times between a call-out on the Malone Road and the Springfield Road.

There was a significant crisis in identity and this was being perpetuated by the low number of police officers emanating from staunchly Republican and Loyalist working class communities. There is a lack of representation within the PSNI from those within working class Republican and Loyalist communities. This has been illustrated through two recent news articles, with one noting that the PSNI had not recruited one person from the Loyalist Shankill Road area of Belfast in five years (Newsletter, 11.04.08), while the second stipulated that there had only been 28 new recruits from Republican dominated West Belfast in the last five years (Andersonstown News, 28.06.08). The issues facing the PSNI in Northern Ireland are not unlike those experienced by police officers in Glasgow, Liverpool and London where there are sections of the working class populations who have disengaged from the policing structures (Johnston et al, 2000). Therefore the PSNI in coming years may look to policing plans and initiatives in cities in England and Scotland to examine their impact at facilitating relationships and forging a link between working class disillusioned communities and the police.

Perceptions of policing

Initially communities had a degree of optimism around policing and the proposed benefits it would bring in relation to addressing criminality, anti-social behaviour and community safety issues. Throughout the conflict normal policing was but an aspiration, but since the conclusion of the Troubles there was a perception that the PSNI would finally have an opportunity to police without paramilitary threats and intimidation. However, recently there has been growing discontent with aspects of policing, with specific attention focusing on response times, attitudes of officers, the flow of information and the following up of call-outs. The realities of policing are not what the communities envisaged. However, the PSNI contend that they are delivering a fair and positive service whilst contending with a continued dissident threat and increased budget constraints.

Furthermore, there has been some degree of criticism from the local communities about the concept of community policing. To a certain extent there appears to be a lack of knowledge within the community as to the aims and objectives of community policing. Essentially, they don't understand the rationale behind its implementation, how its success is measured, or the supposed benefits to their communities. This view reflects the work of Wilson and Kelling (1982) who contend that within the context of effective community policing it requires an understanding of the different communities' expectations and values towards police practice. According to local communities the PSNI are not delivering on the expectations set down by the community, which may explain the apparent lack of support for the idea of community policing.

Public Prosecution Service

Both Loyalist and Republican communities were united in their criticism of the PPS. Their main concerns centred on the lack of knowledge about the organisation and whom it was accountable to. It was interesting to note that for many the PPS and the PSNI were viewed as the same organisation and if decisions went against the community that were the responsibility of the PPS, the PSNI were more than likely to receive the criticism. There has been other independent criticism of the PPS and the manner in which it engages with the public. The recent inspection by the Criminal Justice Inspectorate (CJI, 2007) concluded that there was a need to develop a more productive working relationship with the other criminal justice partners. Furthermore, it was noted that cases were taking too long to progress through the system, and that there were issues around the publishing of case outcomes and providing more comprehensive explanations to victims of the reasons why decisions are taken not to prosecute.

In this new dispensation of policing, encouraging the community to both participate in and actively engage in the sharing of information is crucial if the PSNI are to fulfil their roles and responsibilities. However, the current inconsistencies surrounding prosecutions and sentencing, along with the distinct lack of explanations on the decision-making process, has the potential to damage both the image of the PSNI and the wider criminal justice system.

Summary

The research has drawn together a number of interesting findings that offer an analysis of the central issues facing the delivery of a positive policing service. The question being asked is whether in a post-conflict society such as Northern Ireland there is more of an opportunity to engage with and develop positive working partnerships with a community that has never worked with the formal criminal justice system, as opposed to a community that historically had a strong association with the agencies of law and order but has seen a recent deterioration in the relationship? The research suggests that neither Loyalists nor Republicans have a strong affiliation or identity with the policing structures. If anything there is more expectancy from the

Republican community, however there is a danger that if these expectations are not met then the community's confidence, trust and respect for the organisation will begin to diminish. Within Loyalism there appear to be fewer strategic structures in place to support the communities in embracing the recent reforms to policing. Interestingly, any form of discussion is being generated at the grass roots level. In the absence of political leadership individuals from within these communities are interacting with the policing structures, debating community concerns and attempting to facilitate further conversations which encompass larger sections of their community.

Class appears to be a growing factor in relation to policing. Historically, policing was assessed along Protestant and Catholic lines of demarcation. Complaints surrounded discrimination on the basis of community background, and the organisation was constantly attempting to offer a position of neutrality. The Patten recommendations have gone some way to address these issues with 50:50 recruitment and the development of measures of accountability and transparency. However, to some extent programmes and initiatives continue to be viewed along the lines of community background. NIPB surveys continue to measure views and perceptions of policing and criminal justice on the basis of religion and community background. It is extremely difficult if not impossible to extrapolate the class of respondents, which as the findings from this report indicate, is more important in relation to PSNI engagement than whether you are a Unionist/Loyalist or Nationalist/Republican. Until the criminal justice system at a strategic level begins to think outside the box and redefines the context of policing in Northern Ireland through class and not just community background, then we will not have a police service that has the ability to develop sustainable working partnerships with all areas of society.

On a final note, it is important to recognise how far we all have come in the last decade. Even the most optimistic of individuals would be hard pressed to admit to forecasting the significant changes Northern Ireland has gone through since the paramilitary ceasefires in 1994. Policing was always viewed as one of the most significant obstacles to the conclusion of a violent conflict. Decisions around the implementation of a police service recognised and endorsed by the entire community have proved sensitive and emotional. Each of the main protagonists has had to make courageous sacrifices, faced internal criticisms and altered their own objectives so that society can move on.

9. References

Adams, G (2007) *Speech at Sinn Féin Ard Fheis*, 29.01.07. www.sinnfein.ie.

Auld, J., Gormally, B., McEvoy, K., and Ritchie, M. (1997), *Designing a System of Restorative Justice in Northern Ireland (The Blue Book)*. The Authors, Belfast.

Bell, C (1996) Alternative Justice in Ireland. In Dawson, N., Greer, D. and Ingram, P (eds.). *One Hundred and Fifty Years of Irish Law*. SLS Publications, Belfast.

Bennett-Sandler, G (1979) Citizen participation in policing: Issues in the social control of a social control agency. In Lacovetta, R. and Chang, D. (eds.) *Critical issues in criminal justice*. Durham, North Carolina, Carolina Academic Press.

Brewer, J and Magee, K (1991) *Inside the RUC: Routine Policing in a Divided Society*. Oxford, Clarendon Press.

Brewer, J (1994) *Black and Blue: Policing in South Africa*. Oxford, Clarendon Press.

Brewer, J.D., Lockhart, B., Rodgers, P. (1998) Informal Social Control and Crime Management in Belfast. *British Journal of Sociology*. No 49 (4), 570-585.

Bryan, D (2000) *Orange Parades: The Politics of Ritual, Tradition and Control*. London, Pluto Press.

Byrne, J (2005) *Interface Violence in East Belfast during 2002: the impact on residents of Short Strand and Inner East Belfast*. Belfast, ICR.

Cameron Report (1969) *Disturbances in Northern Ireland: Report of the Cameron Commission Appointed by the Governor of Northern Ireland*. Belfast, HMSO.

Cavanaugh, K.A (1997) Interpretations of political violence in ethnically divided societies. *Terrorism and Political Violence*. No 9 (3), 33-54.

Community Engagement Strategy (2008) *Community Engagement: A strategy for gaining the co-operation of the public with the police in preventing crime*. Belfast, NIPB.

Conway, P (1997) A response to paramilitary policing in Northern Ireland. *Critical Criminology*. No 8 (1), 109-121.

Cory Collusion Inquiry (2004) *Cory Inquiry Collusion Report – Pat Finucane*. London, HMSO.

Cory Collusion Inquiry (2004) *Cory Inquiry Collusion Report – Robert Hamill*. London, HMSO.

Cory Collusion Inquiry (2004) *Cory Inquiry Collusion Report – Rosemary Nelson*. London, HMSO.

Cory Collusion Inquiry (2004) *Cory Inquiry Collusion Report – Billy Wright.* London, HMSO.

Criminal Justice Inspectorate Northern Ireland (2007) *An inspection of the Public Prosecution Service for Northern Ireland.* Belfast, CJINI.

Criminal Justice Inspectorate Northern Ireland (2007) *Northern Ireland Alternatives: Report of an inspection with a view to accreditation under the Government's Protocol for Community Based Restorative Justice.* Belfast, CJINI.

Criminal Justice Inspectorate Northern Ireland (2008) *Community Restorative Justice Ireland: Report of an inspection.* Belfast, CJINI.

Dillon, M (1991) *The Dirty War.* London, Arrow.

Dominique, O (2003) Security-sector restructuring in Bosnia-Herzegovina: addressing the division? *Conflict, Security and Development,* 3 (1): 73-95.

Dunn, S and Morgan, V (1994) *Protestant Alienation in Northern Ireland: A Preliminary Study.* Coleraine, University of Ulster.

Ellison, G (1998) *Youth, Policing and Victimisation in Northern Ireland: Reforming the Royal Ulster Constabulary.* University of Ulster, Economic and Social Research Council.

Ellison, G and Smyth, J (2000) *The Crowned Harp: Policing Northern Ireland.* London, Pluto Press.

Feenan, D. (2002) Community Justice in Conflict: Paramilitary Punishment in Northern Ireland. In Feenan, D (ed) *Informal Criminal Justice.* Ashgate, Aldershot.

Gardiner Committee (1975) *Report of a Committee to Consider, in the Context of Civil Liberties and Human Rights, Measures to Deal with Terrorism in Northern Ireland.* London, HMSO.

Gillespie, G (2008) *Historical Dictionary of the Northern Ireland Conflict.* USA, Scarecrow Press, INC.

Greer, S and White, A (1986) *Abolishing the Diplock Courts: The Case for Restoring Jury Trial to Scheduled Offences in Northern Ireland.* London, Cobden Trust.

Hamilton, J., Radford, K. and Jarman, N (2003) *Policing, Accountability and Young People.* Belfast, ICR.

Hamilton, J., Bell, J., Hanson, U. and Toucas, S (2008) *Segregated Lives: Social division, sectarianism and everyday life in Northern Ireland.* Belfast, ICR.

Hamilton, M (2001) *Working Relationships: An evaluation of community mobile phone networks in Northern Ireland.* Belfast, Community Relations Council.

Helsinki Watch (1993) *Northern Ireland: Human Rights Abuses by All Sides.* No 5 (6). New York, Human Rights Watch.

Human Rights Watch/Helsinki (1991) *Human Rights in Northern Ireland.* New York, HRW.

Hunt Committee (1969) *Report of the Advisory Committee on Police in Northern Ireland.* Belfast, HMSO.

Include Youth (2008) *Evaluation of the North Belfast Young Voices Programme.* Belfast, Include Youth.

Independent Monitoring Report (2005) *Fourth report of the independent monitoring commission.* London, HMSO.

Independent International Commission on Decommissioning (2005) Report of the Independent International Commission on Decommissioning. Belfast, IICD.

http://cain.ulst.ac.uk/events/peace/decommission.

Inquiry into the Devolution of Policing and Justice Matters (2008) *Report into devolution of policing and justice matters.* Stormont, Northern Ireland Assembly.

Jarman, N and Bryan, D (1996) *Parade and Protest: A discussion of parading disputes in Northern Ireland.* Coleraine, The Centre for the Study of Conflict.

Jarman, N and O'Halloran, C (2000) *Peacelines or Battlefields: Responding to violence in interface areas.* Belfast, Community Development Centre North Belfast.

Kelling, G. and Wilson, J. (1982) *Broken Windows: The police and neighbourhood safety.* Atlantic Monthly.

Kennedy, L (1995) Nightmares within Nightmares: Paramilitary repression within working class communities. In: Kennedy, L (ed.) *Crime and Punishment in West Belfast.* The Summer School, Belfast.

Koci, A (1998) Reform of the police in Hungary and Lithuania: empirical findings on the policing of public order. *The European Journal of Social Sciences,* 11 (3): 307-315.

McEvoy, K (2001) Human Rights, Humanitarian Interventions and Paramilitary Activities in Northern Ireland. In: Harvey, C. J. (2001) *Human Rights, Equality and Democratic Renewal in Northern Ireland.* Oxford, Hart Publishing.

McEvoy, K., Mika, H (2002) Republican hegemony or community ownership? Community restorative justice in Northern Ireland. In: Feenan, D. (ed) (2002) *Informal Criminal Justice.* Ashgate, Aldershot.

McGarry, J and O'Leary, B (1999) *Policing Northern Ireland: Proposals for a new start.* Belfast, The Blackstaff Press.

McGloin, J.M. (2003) Shifting Paradigms: Policing in Northern Ireland. *Policing: An International Journal of Strategies and Management,* 1: 118-143.

MacGinty, R and Darby, J (2002) *Guns and Government: The Management of the Northern Ireland Peace Process.* London, Palgrave.

Maesschalck, J (2002) When do scandals have an impact on policy making? A case study of the police reform following the Dutrox scandal in Belgium. *International Public Management Journal* Vol 5: Issue 2: 169-193.

McKittrick, D., Kellers, S., Feeney, B., and Thorton, C (2007) *Lost Lives: The stories of the men, women and children who died as a result of the Northern Ireland troubles.* Edinburgh, Mainstream Publishing Company.

Mika, H (2006) *Community-based Restorative Justice in Northern Ireland.* Belfast, Queens University.

Monaghan, R (2002) 'The Return of Captain Moonlight': Informal Justice in Northern Ireland. *Studies in Conflict and Terrorism.* No 25: 41-56.

Moran, J (2008) *Policing the peace in Northern Ireland: Politics, crime and security after the Belfast Agreement.* Manchester, University Press.

Mulcahy, A (2006) *Policing Northern Ireland: Conflict, legitimacy and reform.* England, Willan Publishing.

Mulcahy, A and Ellison, G (2001) 'The language of policing and the struggle for legitimacy in Northern Ireland', *Policing and Society,* 11 (3-4): 383-404.

NISRA (2008) *Perceptions of Crime: Findings from the 2006/07 Northern Ireland* Crime Survey. Belfast, NIO.

Northern Ireland Policing Board (2007) *Public Perceptions of the Police and the Northern Ireland Policing Board.* Belfast, NIPB.

Northern Ireland Policing Board (2007) *Policing Board Chairman Professor Sir Desmond Rea briefs Members of the Turkish Human Rights Presidency and Human Rights Board.* Belfast, NIPB.

Northern Ireland Policing Board (2007) *Arab/Israeli visit to Northern Ireland Policing Board.* Belfast, NIPB.

Northern Ireland Policing Board (2007) *Hong Kong senior police officers attend meeting.* Belfast, NIPB.

Northern Ireland Policing Board (2008) *Policing Board welcomes Iraqi Parliamentary delegation.* Belfast, NIPB.

Oversight Commissioner for Northern Ireland (2007) *Overseeing the Proposed Revisions for the Policing Services of Northern Ireland – Report 19.* Belfast, Office of the Oversight Commissioner.

O'Doherty, M. (1998) *The Trouble with Guns: Republican Strategy and the Provisional IRA.* Blackstaff Press, Belfast.

O'Mahony, D., Geary, R., McEvoy, K., and Morrison, J., (2000) *Crime, Community and Locale. The Northern Ireland Communities Crime Survey.* Ashgate, Aldershot.

O'Rawe, M. and Moore, L. (1997) *Human Rights on Duty: Principles for better policing – International lessons for Northern Ireland.* Belfast, CAJ.

Patten Report (1999) *A new Beginning: Policing in Northern Ireland. The Report of the Independent Commission on Policing in Northern Ireland.* Belfast, Stationery Office.

Peake, G. (2004) *Policing the peace: Police reform experiences in Kosovo, Southern Serbia and Macedonia.* London, Saferworld.

Police Ombudsman for Northern Ireland (2007) *Statement by the Police Ombudsman for Northern Ireland on her investigation into the circumstances surrounding the death of Raymond McCord Junior and related matters.* Belfast, PONI.

Powell, J. (2007) *Great Hatred, Little Room: Making peace in Northern Ireland.* London, The Bodley Head.

PSNI (2002) *Policing with the Community in Northern Ireland.* Belfast, PSNI.

PSNI (2008) *Chief Constable's Annual Report 2007-2008.* Belfast, PSNI.

Pustintsev, B. (2000) Police reform in Russia: obstacles and opportunities. *Policing and Society.* 10 (1): 79-91.

Reiner, R (1995) Community policing in England and Wales. In Brodeur, J-P. (Ed) *Comparisons in Policing: An International Perspective.* Avebury, Aldershot.

Rose, R (1976) *Northern Ireland: A Time for Change.* London, Macmillan.

Rosenbaum, D. and Lurigio, A. (2000) An inside look at community policing reform – definitions, organisational changes, and evaluation findings. In Alpert, G. and Piquero, A. (eds.) *Community policing – contemporary readings.* Prospect Heights, Illinois: Waveland Press.

Royal Ulster Constabulary (1996) *A Fundamental Review of Policing: Summary and Key Findings.* Belfast, RUC.

Ruane, J and Todd, J (1996) *The Dynamics of Conflict in Northern Ireland.* Cambridge, Cambridge University Press.

Ryder, C (2000) *The RUC (1922-2000) A Force Under Fire.* London, Arrow Books.

Scarman Tribunal (1972) *Violence and Civil Disturbances in Northern Ireland in 1969: Report of Tribunal of Inquiry.* Belfast, HMSO.

Scarman, Lord (1981) *The Scarman Report: The Brixton Disorders.* London, HMSO.

Silke, A. (1999), 'Rebel's Dilemma: The Changing Relationship between the IRA, Sinn Fein and Paramilitary Vigilantism in Northern Ireland', *Terrorism and Political Violence,* 11: 55-99.

Sluka, J.A (1989) *Hearts and Minds, Water and Fish: Support for the IRA and INLA in a Northern Irish Ghetto.* Greenwich, CTR, JAI Press.

Smyth, J (2002) *Community policing and the reform of the Royal Ulster Constabulary.* Belfast, Queens University.

Stalker, J (1988) *The Stalker Affair.* London, Penguin.

Stevens Report (2003) in The Guardian 'Collusion, murder and cover-up'. www.guardian.co.uk 18.04.03

Taylor, P. (1999) *Loyalists.* London, Bloomsbury.

The Agreement (1998) *The Agreement: its your decision.* Belfast, NIO.

Tomlinson, M (1993) Policing the new Europe: the Northern Ireland factor. In Bunyan, T. (ed.) *Statewatching the new Europe*. London, Statewatch.

Weitzer, R (1995) *Policing under fire: Ethnic Conflict and Police Community Relations in Northern Ireland*. Albany, Suny Press.

Winston, T (1997) Alternatives to Punishment Beatings and Shootings in a Loyalist Community in Belfast. *Critical Criminology*, 8: 1.

Winston, T., Watters, D. and Drummond, B. (1999) *Shankill Alternatives*. Fortnight, September: 18-19.